Do You Love Me?

Exploring Our Relationships with God and Others

DEBBIE SWINDOLL

Activities by Monica Romig Green

GRAFTED LIFE
MINISTRIES
Becoming One with Christ

TABLE OF CONTENTS

Dear friends,

Welcome to *Do You Love Me?* I am excited for what you will experience in the next few weeks. This short book is designed to engage you in relationship with God and others. You will notice that the text contains a variety of invitations—to meditate, to read, to pray, to act, to dialogue with others—which you can accept as you feel led and able.

There are no requirements for engagement, just opportunities to be refreshed. Allow this journey to enliven your vision for what is possible when relating with God and others. Feel free to pause on ideas that intrigue you and to participate in activities that recharge you. You will find explanations for each activity as you go along which will guide you through the process.

So let's get started. I know that God is traveling with you. May you feel His blessing as you begin.

Debbie

Debbie Swindoll

How to Use This Book

This workbook is written for group or individual use over a suggested four week period. Each week has additional activities alongside the text of *Do You Love Me?* to bring the experience into your daily prayers and conversations.

Rest and Receive

Each week opens with several short activities for you to relax with and take in, like a deep breath.

The **Opening Prayer** focuses your heart and reminds you that God is present as you think and read.

The five recorded **Scripture Meditations**, one for each day of the week, invite you to ruminate on God's Word. Each recording is about 5 minutes long. We created these meditations to let you listen to Scripture spoken aloud and receive rest.

Read Access Online Content on page 9 for instruction on how to download and listen to these meditations.

Read and Reflect

Do You Love Me? presents concepts from Scripture through engaging stories and clear explanations. The book is divided into ten short chapter selections, followed by questions for personal reflection.

Use the questions in **Pause to Consider** to prayerfully reflect on how what you are learning touches your life. We've provided you with open space to write out your answers to help solidify your thoughts and conclusions.

Live Into It

Following the reading, we've included three 20-minute activities that encourage you to try out the ideas of the book. We recommend these activities as an accessible starting place for experiencing *Do You Love Me?* in the context of your daily life.

Discuss Together

Each week ends with questions for group discussion, carefully chosen to help spark lively dialogue with others who are reading *Do You Love Me?*

We pray that as you engage with this workbook, your life will be impacted as you grow in love for our Lord Jesus Christ and His church.

Access Online Content

This workbook comes with additional online resources meant to deepen your experience of *Do You Love Me?* You can download these resources on the publisher's website and listen to them on your computer or mobile device.

How to Access Online Content

» Visit www.graftedlife.org and log in with an existing account, or register a new account. You can create a free account using the "Member Login" menu on the main navigation bar.

» From the account dashboard, click to "Add Online Content."

» Input the following case-sensitive code: AXU8V2SE

» Bookmark www.graftedlife.org/podcasts for quick access.

Week 1

In the beginning was the Word, and the Word was with God,
and the Word was God. He was in the beginning with God.
All things were made through him, and without him was not
any thing made that was made.

In him was life, and the life was the light of men. The light
shines in the darkness, and the darkness has not overcome it.

John 1:1-5

Rest and Receive

Opening Prayer

Find a quiet place to relax where you will not be disturbed by others. Set aside any items which might vie for your attention. Consider God's presence with the following prayer:

Lord *God,*

I pause to acknowledge that You are with me right now
Even though I may not feel or recognize Your presence.

Help me to grasp Your desire for relationship
And to listen for whatever you want to reveal to me.

I entrust myself to You.

In the name of Jesus, Amen.

Scripture Meditations

We have recorded five meditations on the following biblical passages to draw your attention to God throughout the week. Access these recordings at www.graftedlife.org/podcasts (see page 9).

Monday	John 1:1-5
Tuesday	Matthew 11:28-30
Wednesday	Genesis 1:26-27
Thursday	John 3:19-20
Friday	Romans 8:19-22

READ AND REFLECT

Preface to Do You Love Me?

Several years ago my spiritual life derailed. After decades of try-ing to live according to the Bible, I "woke up" exhausted one day confronted with the words of Christ in Matthew 11:28-30—"Come to me, all who labor and are heavy laden, and I will give you rest. Take my yoke upon you, and learn from me, for I am gentle and lowly in heart, and you will find rest for your souls. For my yoke is easy, and my burden is light" (ESV). As I let those verses contrast with the true state of my internal life, I concluded that if Christ's invitation was true, then I was doing something fundamentally wrong in my walk with Him.

The cry of my heart became, "LORD, teach me how these words of Yours can be true in my life." This prayer was a turning point in my spiritual journey. It was as if I got off a derailed train and onto another, only I had no idea where the new train was going or how it worked. I could only hope that the journey would feel less burdensome and that the destination would indeed be a place of rest for my tired soul.

In the years since that spiritual wake-up call, I have studied and experienced many things that have influenced my understanding of the gospel. God has helped me discover new ways to engage in the journey of sanctification. My knowledge of how the new train operates and how I can know, love, and learn from the gentle and humble-hearted Engineer has grown. I now understand that lasting change doesn't result when I exhaust myself through trying harder to be good, but rather when I bring my brokenness into a relationship with Christ.

That relationship has transformed my life. What I have learned over the last fifteen years has convinced me that our spiritual growth rests on the quality of our relationship with God. My goal in these pages is to share my experience and to highlight biblical ideas about the sanctification journey that have helped me grasp the reality of Christ's invitation to live in His yoke.

If God uses these words to encourage you about the possibilities of abiding in a close relationship with Him, then that result will be to His glory, empowered by His Spirit, who is always calling us closer to the Father's heart.

Chapter 1. Why Relationship?

I grew up in the evangelical church. I believed in Jesus as my savior at an early age. As a young Christian, I heard Christianity commonly described as "having a personal relationship with Christ," and I often used this description, myself. Looking back, I think I understood that phrase primarily from a conversion perspective. I equated the "personal relationship" to my initial decision to accept Jesus as the Savior for my sins. I knew that everyone had to make this individual choice in order to come into the faith. But the majority of my experience after my conversion moment didn't feel like an abiding relationship with a Person. I operated independently, doing what I could to obey and conform to the Christian image that I read about in the Bible. My concern was to be good, to avoid guilt and the feeling that my behavior might disappoint God. I had little awareness of God's presence with me and little knowledge of what an interactive relationship with God might look like.

I believe there was a part of me that wanted a different spiritual experience—a deep and quiet longing to know God intimately, or as the Apostle Paul writes, to be known by God (Gal. 4:9). But if I am honest, there were other parts of me that appreciated the distance, that feared being close to God. I felt comfort in controlling the journey and dreaded what God might ask me to do or give up if I got too close. I avoided these feelings. They didn't make logical sense in light of what I knew in my head about God—His love and the length that He was willing to go to save me. I had no idea how to explore the disparity between what I knew about God and the fear that often emerged from my heart.

But God planned so much more for me. After my spiritual life derailed, God began to awaken me to the truth that my definition of "personal relationship" was only the embryo of what He had in mind when it came to relating with me. My understanding limited my spiritual growth and exhausted me. In contrast, the gospel actually offered me the opportunity to grow in intimacy, trust and love for God, to enjoy the privileges of being in His family, to become His friend. His relationship with me was meant to invade every aspect and activity of my life.

Sometimes in life we have these insightful moments—when something that we think we know takes on new meaning or is nuanced in a life-changing way. The potential to have an ongoing relationship with God was like that for me. Once the idea was planted it continued to expand and eventually gave me a framework that made everything else in my Christian life fit together. It has taken time for God to reorient my mind and heart and help me understand His desires for me. One thing I needed to grasp was how important relationship is to God.

God desires relationship simply because He relates. One of the most mysterious realities about the personhood of God is the truth that He is Triune. Relationship abides within His Being. Scripture gives evidence to this important doctrine of the Church. For example, the Bible describes God as the "Us" that made man in His image and then had to expel those first image-bearers, Adam and Eve, from the Garden of Eden after their sin (Gen. 1:26, 3:22). The New Testament explains how God's plan of redemption and sanctification is carried out through God's cooperative work in the Trinity as Father, Son, and Spirit share the same will for us and constantly communicate within their Being to bring that will to fruition (John 14, Rom. 8:12-39).

Without dividing His essence, there is communication, association, unity, understanding, and community between the persons of the Father, the Son, and the Spirit. There is perfect, divine, eternal relationship. The doctrine of the Trinity informs us that relationship is fundamental to the nature of God. The Triune Personhood of God defines, initiates, establishes and sustains the concept of relationship. It is the starting point.

God extends relationship because He loves. God is a lover. The Apostle John describes Him as love (1 John 4:8). This relational truth about God is also a part of His Personhood. God loves first within the Godhead. As the Trinity demonstrates, relationship is more perfectly expressed in the giving and receiving of love. Jesus explained that His unity with and adherence to the Father's will was proof of His love for the Father (John 14:31).

God also demonstrated His love beyond the Trinity and established the framework in which He intended all other relationships to function. For example, He expressed His love and extended relationship to His creation through the goodness of His original design. He exhibited His love in relationship with Adam and Eve in the Garden of Eden (Gen. 1-3). After the Fall, He continued to display His love to the ancient nations by instituting an unconditional covenant with Abraham and his descendants, guaranteeing His ultimate faithfulness to them (regardless of their fickleness toward Him) with the promise to bring blessing to the whole world (Gen. 12,15). He demonstrated His great love for us in that while we were still sinners and enemies He sent His Son to die so that He might restore us to a loving relationship with Him (Rom. 5:6-11). In sending Jesus, He also lovingly kept His promise to bring blessing to the world. (In the next section, we will further explore the relational dynamics recorded in Scripture.)

God is *always* relating and loving. Stop and think about that. That truth is not just a sound theological idea, but a reality that has the potential to transform our days—to invite us to participate in an ongoing relationship with Him. We can enter into that relationship because of Christ. For those who believe in Him, His life, death, and resurrection restore our relationship with God. It is now possible for us to accept the love of God and to love Him in return—to consistently engage in acts of healthy relationship and to be an abiding part of the on-going love exchange of the Trinity (John 15:1-11).

This is something that God has always wanted for us and from us. In fact it is not just an optional add-on for the super spiritual, but a direct command from our Creator. Scripture gives preeminence to the idea of relating to God by requiring that we love God with our heart, soul, mind, and strength and by positioning love as the foundation of the whole law (Deut. 6:5, Matt. 22:37-38). The scope of such a command goes far beyond the realm of trying to be good by following rules and avoiding feelings of guilt or disappointment. This scriptural imperative requires that we honestly explore our thoughts, emotions, desires, attitudes, and actions before God in order to relate with Him from the depths of our hearts (Jer. 31:31-34, Eph. 3:14-19).

Does abiding with God in such an intimate way sound like the kind of "personal relationship" you desire? If you are like me, it may not be what you originally understood when you became a Christian. Through the rest of this book, we will explore God's invitation to engage deeply with Him in a relationship that will transform our lives.

PAUSE TO CONSIDER

» When you think of God, do you think of Him in the ways described above—as constantly and continually relating to you and
the world in love? How would you personally describe God's
point-of-view regarding relationship with you and the world?

Sometimes I feel like its personal
& sometimes hands off, Part of me
wonders why anyone would want a
relationship with me.

» What does your relationship with God look like on a day-to-day
basis? How involved is God in your life?

I try & trying more lately to involve or
or reach out or be mindful of God
throughout the day. I guess mostly
I don't think of Him being involved
in my life

» Are you satisfied with your relationship with God? What aspects
bring you great satisfaction, joy, comfort, or gratitude? What
aspects are difficult, disappointing, troublesome, or simply
non-existent?

Not satisfied in general. Glad & satisfied
that he is in charge, his word bring
some comfort, that he came into my life
& totally changed it
But I wish there was more intimacy
with Him
Sometimes I feel like its a task — the relationship
w/ God than natural

» Take a moment to talk with God about your relationship with Him. What would you like to express to Him? How would you desire Him to respond? Take a moment to journal your thoughts.

Chapter 2. Going Back to the Beginning

I was greatly encouraged to understand that God desires and invites me into relationship with Him, but knowing how to respond in love to God was, at times, a frustrating exercise. It takes two to be in a relationship. I didn't come preprogrammed to understand how to accept God's invitation. I struggled to know how to engage with a Spirit. As I mentioned earlier, there were parts of me that were reluctant to be close with God. It seemed as if I had fundamental heart problems that were getting in the way of intimacy with God. Not only did I need to have my understanding of God's views on relationship expanded, but I also needed to grow in awareness of my heart's true condition, particularly about the hindrances inside me that kept me from desiring a deeper relationship with Him.

Desire was not my only problem, though. I also had relational habits that hampered healthy interactions with others. I come from a family that functioned in its unique brokenness. All of our families do to some degree. I continue to grow, with the help of God and others, to understand how that brokenness and my own sinfulness affect me, creating wounded places in me that impact the ways that I relate with others. But back in the day, I had a certain naivety about how deeply my relational deficiencies impacted my life and was ignorant about how they disrupted my relationship with God.

Thankfully, God's grace comes in many different packages. Often when He invites us to a deeper relationship, He allows us to feel the insufficiencies of our current one. Along with persistent feelings of exhaustion during my spiritual derailment, God invited me to experience how poorly I was operating in all my relationships. My kids, who were teenagers at the time, were particularly useful tools in the hand of God. They often told me or showed me the shallowness of my relational capacities.

I desired for them to be good, to obey, and to be involved in church. I wanted them to do all the things that I thought God wanted me to do. But just like me, they had deeper issues in their hearts and because I didn't know how to explore my deeper issues, I was incapable of being with them or helping them to know how to explore theirs. I didn't often talk with them about their feelings. I defaulted to lecturing them and giving them advice. I was quick to deal with their problems, rather than to be with them. Their unresolved troubles made me uncomfortable, and I didn't want to feel my inadequacy. Over time God allowed me to see that my relational shallowness was not just affecting my interactions with my kids, but that it stemmed from a lack of depth in my relationship with Him.

I needed a relational overhaul and an honest understanding of what was happening inside of me. I believe God made me aware of these failures so that I would be willing to enter into a new journey with Him. In the midst of my dysfunction, God brought me into a community of believers who walked with me, helping me to discover Him and myself in deeper ways. He also showed me over and over through the pages of Scripture how deeply He desires a relationship with me. The stories of the Bible became alive with relevant illustrations about the struggles of my heart.

The Bible has a lot to say about relationships. A main purpose of Scripture seems to be to reveal the nature of God's relationship with the human race which He created in His image. Scripture also provides understanding about people's relationships with each other and our responsibilities in connection with the rest of creation. From its opening chapters which contrast the picture of relational harmony in the Garden of Eden with the devastating relational dysfunction which resulted from the Fall, the Scriptures illustrate both the benefits of living with God and the consequences of living independently (in human pride) from God's design.

Over the next few chapters, we will explore some of what the Bible reveals about relationships. As we do, there will be places to stop, reflect, and talk with God about how these scriptural ideas help us understand our lives.

CREATION'S STANDARD

When I hear the name "Garden of Eden," it evokes ethereal images in my imagination. Natural beauty, an environment of abundance, and a sense of ease in life are all concepts that play through my mind. Who of us hasn't longed for a glimpse of Eden or the opportunity to go back in time and experience, even for a day, the reflected glory of such a place?

Although we cannot experience it personally, reflecting on the garden narrative affords us the opportunity to ponder the relational dynamic recorded between God and Adam. We can see a picture of God's desire to relate to us and how we were created to relate to Him.

The creation story unveils the deep affection and care that God demonstrated in providing the heavens and earth for the sustenance and enjoyment of man, who He positioned as the culmination of His creative activity. God brought Adam to life with His own breath (Gen. 2:7). God honored the first couple with the responsibility of dominion over the rest of creation (Gen. 1:26-31). God expresses

His personal connection with man by fashioning both men and women after His image. Part of the image of God that is instilled in humanity is the ability to relate—to participate in relationships where love is exchanged.

Within just a few verses, Scripture portrays an open and ongoing relationship between God and Adam. Adam received instruction from God about his vocational responsibilities and about a prohibition God placed on his activities. God invited Adam to participate in naming the animals and blessed him with the gift of a perfectly compatible human partner (Gen. 2:15-25). By creating Eve for Adam and by commenting that it was not good for man to be alone, God again affirms how much He values relationship.

God's visitations with Adam and Eve in the cool of the day characterized their relationship with Him. Scripture implies that Adam and Eve recognize the sound of God walking in the garden, which leads us to conclude they were familiar with this experience with God (Gen. 3:8). The relational context appears loving, open, innocent, and ongoing.

Sin and the Relational Fallout

Many times I have wished for more information about Adam and Eve's experience in the Garden of Eden prior to the fateful day recorded in Genesis 3. Scripture introduces their fall from glory so suddenly that as readers, we barely get our bearings before the narrative turns our perspective upside down. As Scripture explores Adam and Eve's actions that day, we begin to see what caused the break in humankind's relationship with God. Reflecting on their encounter with God is valuable not only to understand the nature of sin but to recognize the relational damage that resulted from it and which continues to plague us today.

Genesis 3 begins by introducing another of God's creatures, a serpent that was superior in wit to the other beasts of the field. Scripture records a conversation between the serpent and Eve in which he tempts her to eat from the only tree that God had banned. The serpent's arguments for disregarding what God had said strike at the heart of Eve's relationship with God. Through crafty questioning and half-truths, the serpent leads Eve to consider the possibility that God's word is not true and that God's plan for Eve will not enable her to reach her highest potential (Gen. 3:1-5). If these charges proved true, God would not be a trustworthy Being to relate with intimately and dependently.

At the center of this temptation lay a relational decision: to love God by trusting His plan, following His instructions, and enjoying the bounty of His provision, or to compete with God by seeking the wisdom gained from eating the forbidden fruit as a way to operate in equality with God. Eating the fruit offered a chance to become autonomous—independent from God—but would also be an unfaithful rejection of the couple's current loving relationship with Him. We all know what Eve and Adam ultimately decided.

In a real sense, their relational choice is at the heart of all sin. We don't often like to think that our behaviors have relational significance or meaning. The essence of sin, however, is choosing self-rule over surrender to the rule of our Creator. This is a relational rejection. It is not just the rejection of an idea, but a lack of trust in God's honesty, goodness, and love. Every sinful act through the ages has had the same rebellious heart posture at its core.

When Adam and Eve chose to reject God and strike out on their own, their choice had devastating relational consequences. When their "eyes were opened" (Gen. 3:7) as the serpent predicted, instead of seeing their own glory revealed on a level equal with God, they were awakened to feelings of exposure and shame from their nakedness. Scripture reveals that they quickly worked to cover themselves with fig-leaf garments. This covering act was the first sign of relational alienation.

Circumstances deteriorated from there. Like a snowball rolling downhill, the relational disintegration between the first couple and God quickly gained momentum. When they heard God coming to meet with them, they physically hid themselves from His presence.

When questioned about their actions, they seemed incapable of honest conversation. They defaulted to half-truths and excuses, deflecting responsibility by blaming each other and even God. The open, innocent, transparent, trusting, and loving environment that characterized their previous relationships in the garden was now gone. The choice against faith—to move away from God and His ways—brought shame and guilt, resulting in the relational dysfunction of covering, hiding, lying, and blaming. This brought relational consequences on every level.

At the most crucial level, Adam and Eve's decision that day brought about the consequence of spiritual death—the dissolution of the natural and normal state of their relationship with God. It separated them from Him. Spiritual death was not an arbitrary punishment for disobedience but the inevitable outcome that God had warned them would follow if they chose to eat that fruit. To think of this act as *simply* disobedient (which it certainly was) is to miss the heart disposition that motivated it and broke the relational bond. Eating the fruit involved distrusting God's will and therefore choosing to live life apart from Him, guided instead by their own wisdom and desires. God's willingness to honor that choice for their lives and the lives of their descendants resulted in the state of humankind's spiritual death.

As children of Adam's race, we experience the consequences of spiritual death. It is no longer natural or normal for us to be in relationship with God. We are born estranged from a dependent connection with Him who created us, left to secure our happiness in our own strength and in the best way that we see fit. The shame and guilt resulting from our sinful choices cause us to cover up our true nature and to hide from God in darkness (John 3:19-20).

In addition it seems we are all plagued with a deep mistrust of God's love and goodness—the same mistrust at the heart of the original temptation. We are easily deceived by the notion that we can attain wisdom or knowledge to figure out life on our own. Deep within our souls we experience the loneliness of life without God, but our ability to distract ourselves often keeps us from feeling the extent of that reality.

Being alienated from God and His love on this fundamental level also spills over into our other relationships. We see the beginning of human family dysfunction in the lives of the first couple. When Adam and Eve ate the forbidden fruit, it fractured more than their relationship with God. It also damaged their ability to function in loving relationship to one another.

Before the Fall, Scripture characterizes Adam and Eve's relationship with each other as one in which they were naked and unashamed. This reality was an expression of relational transparency—the ultimate "what you see is what you get" opportunity without rejection or recrimination. They enjoyed the freedom to function in love and cooperation with each other, accomplishing more as a team than they could as individuals (Gen. 2:18-25).

After they rejected their relationship with God, however, the purity of their relationship with each other changed. Their shame limited their ability to be transparent, and they hid their nakedness from one another. When God questioned them about their actions, Adam, unable to be honest and take responsibility, blamed Eve for his actions. Eve blamed the serpent, and they both insinuated that God was ultimately at fault.

By engaging in blaming, the first couple inflicted each other with relational wounds, breaking the trust between them. No longer freely able to cooperate with each other, they began to compete for happiness. Self-preservation became an instinctive value of their hearts. Rather than thriving in the abundance of God's provision, they were forced through the consequences of their actions (Gen. 3:16-24) to feel the scarcity of what they could provide for themselves. Genesis 4 records the ultimate consequence of human competition and relational wounding: Cain choosing to kill his brother Abel.

In a more subtle sense, the story of the Fall also infers a loss of humans' ability to be in honest relationship with oneself. It appears that Adam and Eve's ability to hide from realities and evade truths not only hurt their relationship with others but also interfered with their own self knowledge (Gen. 3:10-13). Their separation from God marred their self perception, rendering their hearts capable of great self deceit (Jer. 17:9-10).

In addition, Adam and Eve lost touch with their vocational identity. When they followed the advice of the serpent, they failed to rule over creation. Consequently, it became more difficult for them to subdue the earth and cause it to flourish (Gen. 3:17-19). This loss subjected the creation to futility, and it longs for God to reveal the redeemed as His sons so that our glory will free creation from corruption (Rom. 8:19-22).

This last consequence completes the picture of the relational devastation that ensued from the Fall—estrangement from God; the capability to deceive, blame, and hurt each other; and a diminished ability to understand their own hearts and their human vocation. The human chaos recorded in Genesis 4-11 illustrates how these tendencies multiplied in the lives of Adam and Eve's descendants.

Pause to Consider

» How do you see the relational consequences of the Fall playing out in your own life? Have you made a choice for self-rule over God's rule lately? What have been the effects of that choice?

» Do you see the effects of Adam and Eve's inter-relational wounds in your life? Have you recently deceived, blamed, or hurt someone in your life? Has someone deceived, blamed, or hurt you? How have these actions affected your relationship with each other?

» Have you experienced yourself hiding from the truth lately or worrying how others perceive you? Have you recently discovered anything about yourself that was surprising or unexpected?

» What about your vocational role in the world? Do you experience any confusion regarding your identity, purpose, or role? Take a few minutes to journal your thoughts.

Live Into It

Practice Relating to God

Spend 20 minutes intentionally staying aware of God's presence while doing a common everyday task, such as driving, cleaning, watching TV, cooking, etc. If your attention wanders away from God, just gently bring it back without passing judgment on yourself. Notice how easy or difficult this is for you. Notice what seems different for you as you keep God's presence in the forefront of your mind throughout your activity.

Practice Your Vocation over God's Creation

Spend 20 minutes physically caring for some aspect of creation. This could involve tending to a garden (watering, weeding, pruning, planting, etc.), tending to a pet, picking up trash in a park, biking or walking somewhere instead of driving, etc. As you engage in this activity, consider your relationship with God's creation and your role within it. Notice how this compares to your everyday attitude towards God's creation.

Practice Interpersonal Responsibility

Spend 20 minutes thinking about a relationship in your life where there is conflict. Journal about the circumstances that led to and proceeded from the conflict. Consider your part in the conflict, and note where you have contributed to the relational breakdown. Talk with God to determine if there is anything you need to confess to Him and/or to the other person.

NOTES

DISCUSS TOGETHER

What do you think?

How have the readings, questions and Scripture meditations challenged or altered your understanding of relationship with God?

How do you feel?

How do you feel about the current state of your relationships: with God, others, yourself and/or creation?

What about God?

Where do you recognize God's activity in your life? Give everyone a moment to pray silently, so they can talk to God about this question. Then invite everyone to share, if they want to.

Where to go from here?

What might you want to remember from this discussion for the coming week?

NOTES

Week 2

The true light, which gives light to everyone, was coming into the world. He was in the world, and the world was made through him, yet the world did not know him. He came to his own, and his own people did not receive him.

But to all who did receive him, who believed in his name, he gave the right to become children of God, who were born, not of blood nor of the will of the flesh nor of the will of man, but of God.

John 1:9-13

REST AND RECEIVE

Opening Prayer

Find a quiet place to relax where you will not be disturbed by others. Set aside any items which might vie for your attention. Consider God's presence with the following prayer:

Holy God,

You sought me in my sin
And secured me through the precious blood of Jesus.

Your Spirit is my constant Companion and Guide.
Teach me Your love.

Help me understand how to embrace
Your relationship with me.

In Jesus' name, Amen.

Scripture Meditations

We have recorded five meditations on the following biblical passages to draw your attention to God throughout the week. Access these recordings at www.graftedlife.org/podcasts (see page 9).

MONDAY	John 1:9-13
TUESDAY	Genesis 17:1-8
WEDNESDAY	Galatians 4:4-7
THURSDAY	Hebrews 4:14-16
FRIDAY	John 14:15-17

READ AND REFLECT

Chapter 3. God's Heart for Reconciliation

Relational estrangement is counterintuitive to the loving heart, whether that estrangement is physical, emotional, or spiritual. Just recently, I looked into the face of my first grandchild for the first time. When he was born, he lived in southern California and I lived in Dallas, Texas. As I gazed into his precious eyes, I was overwhelmed with the desire to be present in this little boy's life. I spontaneously blurted out, "Wesley, if you will move to Dallas, Grammy will buy you a pony!" It was difficult to imagine missing important moments of his life and not being able to interact with him regularly. I would do almost anything to resolve the physical distance between us.

Although I deeply felt the separation from my grandson, sometimes as an actual physical ache, the reality is that my grandson felt nothing at all. He doesn't understand what he is missing. He would likely go about his life accepting the way it is. I am the one with the longings and the hopes unfulfilled. I carry the relational knowledge and experience of what could be.

My situation with my grandson has afforded me a small glimpse into the heart of God. The first three chapters of Genesis lay the foundation for understanding how the fall of humankind forever severed the relational bond between God and His beloved creation. Adam and Eve tangibly experienced this separation. They could feel the difference between life in the garden with the bounty of God's provision and presence, and life on the other side, struggling in their vocation and living with the grief of broken relationships.

But their descendants, born in sin without prior experience of freely relating with God, knew no difference. They didn't come into the world feeling like the walking dead, understanding the tragedy of their situation. Like them, we are born for the most part accepting life as it is, though at times we feel the struggle and long for something more. God is the one who truly knows the difference. As our Creator, only He carries a true knowledge of what is possible in a relationship with Him. As a relater and lover, He was unwilling to leave the situation without remedy. Humankind's sinfulness disables us from reaching up to God, so God graciously intervenes to reach down.

God has a plan for reconciliation, for life with Him. He wants to save us not only from ultimate death, but also from the way we are currently living life. Throughout the rest of the Bible, God's reconciliation plan methodically unfolds, culminating in the revelation of His Son, Jesus. The inspired writings of His followers illuminate for us the incredible gift of Christ's work. Scripture helps us to grasp the significance of God's invitation for reconciliation. It awakens us to our need and casts a vision for what life with God could be like. Salvation doesn't make sense if you don't understand what you are being saved from, and restoration doesn't seem that important unless you long for that to which you are being restored.

So God relates the story to us. He offers us a way to understand the difference between life on our own and life with Him. Throughout the Old Testament, God tells us the story again and again—sometimes triumphantly and sometimes tragically.

So what are the important points of this story, and how do we see them illustrated in the history of the Old Testament?

First, God affirms that He created us for loving relationship with Him and with others, and that He is committed to pursue the fulfillment of that plan. After the Fall, God continued interacting with men and women. He faithfully started over with humanity even after periods of overt sin and evil. He refused to completely destroy His creation and after the flood, promised never again to destroy the earth in that manner even though the hearts of men are evil from their youth (Gen. 8:20-22). He remained faithful to His relationship with Israel even after they rejected and turned from Him many times. He called them lovingly back into relationship through the words and warnings of the prophets and brought them back to Canaan after their season of exile.

Second, God affirms His love for us and assures us that life with Him is good. One of the key ways that God demonstrates His love is through His covenantal promises. The beauty of covenantal agreements is that it allows God to testify to what He is promising in the relationships. He purposefully makes it clear up front. He lovingly gives people a reason to trust Him by formally stating how He plans to act toward them. He openly communicates the benefits of a relationship with Him and gives people a vision for what is possible if they abide in that relationship. He also outlines any responsibilities that men and women have in the relationship and lets them know if His benefits are conditioned on their responses or not.

In the Old Testament we read of God's covenantal agreements with Noah, Abraham, Moses and the people of Israel, and King David and his descendants. We also read of the promises God made concerning the New Covenant. Each of these covenants gives us an opportunity to learn more about the trustworthiness of God and understand how He has offered men and women throughout history a tangible way to live with Him and experience His love.

Third, God honestly reveals to us the tragedy of life without Him. He tells us why we need to be saved and reconciled to Him and to one another by recording in story after story what happens when people live life out of their own wisdom. He illustrates this through the lifestyles of the heathen nations (Gen. 18-19), and also through those who forsake their relationship with Him. The book of Judges gives several sad examples of what "doing what is right in one's own eyes" can lead to in the lives of those who know God.

The stories of Abraham, his son, and grandson, recorded in the book of Genesis, show us that the effects of the Fall leave human beings with deep heart habits of autonomy—living independently from God. Each of us need to recognize and deal with these relationship-denying tendencies in order to enter into the fullness of

God's instruction to walk before Him, enjoying the blessings of having Him as our God (Gen. 17:1-8).

Through the chronicle of the successes and failures of Israel's relationship with God, we can observe how the quality of that relationship affected the lives of the people (Deut. 28). Israel's history reveals a treasure of truths about God's faithfulness to His relationship with them based on His love and requiring their trust. It also portrays honest and often painful examples of the nation's inability to reciprocate His love well, if at all. These ancient stories offer insight and a relational master class. They introduce many reflective opportunities to those of us serious about knowing God and knowing ourselves in truth. They invite us to humbly see the realities of our own hearts. Ultimately, they lead us to recognize our need for a Savior.

Pause to Consider

» How have you tended to view the stories of the Old Testament? What picture of God tends to form for you when you read the stories? Is it different from your understanding of God as revealed in Jesus Christ?

» As you consider the Old Testament, what specific stories or verses come to mind that speak to God's desire for relationship with His people? Do these encourage you?

» Do you identify with a particular person in the Old Testament? If so, which one? What does that person's story reveal to you about your own heart and your desire for relationship with God? Take a few minutes and journal your thoughts.

Chapter 4. Christ: The Ultimate Reconciler

The Apostle Paul writes in the fourth chapter of Galatians that "when the fullness of time had come, God sent forth his Son, born of a woman, under the law, to redeem those who were under the law, so that we might receive adoption as sons. And because you are sons, God has sent the Spirit of his Son into our hearts, crying,

'Abba! Father!' So you are no longer a slave, but a son, and if a son, then an heir through God" (vv. 4-7).

Jesus, the Son of God, is the ultimate revelation of God's reconciliation plan. The books written about His life, death, and resurrection, recorded in Scripture, are called Gospels. They are stories of good news. On the night that Jesus was born, an angel appeared to shepherds near Bethlehem, proclaiming, "I bring you good news of great joy that will be for all the people. For unto you is born this day in the city of David a Savior, who is Christ the Lord" (Luke 2:10-11).

The Old Testament stories reveal humankind's relationship with God as one of frustration and failure. When we humbly look at this truth, we begin to long for good news. We want the Messiah to appear. We start to grasp why we need a Savior. I think that is part of the beauty of the Bible. The Old Testament prepares our hearts to receive the good news of Jesus.

When I first accepted the good news of Jesus, I was just a little girl. I was attending a Vacation Bible School program at our church. I was the youngest of three children, and I knew that everyone else in my family believed in Jesus. I received a common explanation of the process of becoming a Christian, one which may not be uncommon in these days either. Those who presented the plan of salvation first told me that I was a sinner. I'm sure they explained the term in a way a child would understand. I grasped that I had done bad things and those bad things were causing me to go to hell when I died. But because God loved me, He had sent His Son, Jesus, to die for my sins so that after I died I could live with Him in heaven instead. If I believed in Jesus and accepted Him as my personal Savior, then I would gain eternal life.

It seemed like an obvious choice to me. I didn't want to go to hell. That sounded scary. Besides, the rest of my family was going to heaven, and I didn't want to be alone. I remember to this day some forty-five years later how glad and relieved I was to belong with my family in that way. That was the good news to me. I was not going to be left behind or separated from them.

What I didn't understand that day, or for many decades into my Christian experience, was that Jesus's life, death, and resurrection secured far more than my eternal destiny. It also offered me a chance to be reconciled to God. In essence, He was offering me a chance to feel about God the way I was feeling about my family—to learn to love Him, abide with Him, and never have to be separated from Him again. Jesus had secured a way for me to become a child of God and join His family.

That is truly good news—relational hope for all the people.

Jesus reveals to us just how far God was willing to go to offer us adoption and the reality of a life with Him. One of the more poignant scenes from the Old Testament is found in Genesis 22. The story is a familiar one to many of us: it is the retelling of a time when God tested Abraham. In order to reveal the state of Abraham's trust and love for Him, God asks Abraham to sacrifice his only son Isaac. Abraham is willing, but God stops him before he completes the task, providing a ram for the sacrifice instead. What God didn't require of Abraham, He offered to us as proof of His love and desire to restore us to a relationship with Him. He sacrificed His only Son. Jesus, as a willing participant in the sacrifice, said there is no greater love than this, that a man lay down his life for a friend (John 15:13).

This is such good news if we take advantage of it. But tragically it seems as if Jesus's death reconciled us into a relationship with God that few believers are actually experiencing or enjoying. For many years, reconciliation without relationship was the condition of my life. Now when I read the New Testament, the revelation and on-going ministry of Jesus broaden my vision of the relationship God desires to have with me. If we understand that reality and enter into that relationship, it will begin to change our lives.

Jesus's death does provide the payment for our sins. I understood that correctly as a little girl. But His sacrifice does more than give us a ticket to heaven. It also provides a way for us to constantly engage with God. Unlike the sacrifices of the Jewish law which the priests needed to make repeatedly for the nation's trespasses,

Christ's death was the final sacrifice for sin (Heb. 7:27). Those in relationship with Him are no longer under condemnation (Romans 8:1). We have no need to find our own coverings for sin and shame, as Adam and Eve did in the garden. Christ's righteousness is now our permanent cover. Wearing His righteous clothing allows us to come into the light of His truth and confess our trespasses in the safety of our relationship with Him. (I John 1:5-10). That is where we will find help, mercy, and grace (Heb. 4:14-16). Our sin no longer has the power to separate us from our day-to-day relationship with God.

Jesus also helps us to know God. He is Immanuel, God with us. Relationship requires that those involved know each other, as a basis from which love can flow. Jesus explains the true character of the Father in a personal way. The God who has always existed became flesh for us so that we could comprehend His nature (John 1:1-18, 14:7-11). The same Father that Jesus intimately knew, revealed, and called on, is now our Father. Through Christ we are adopted into a relationship with God, to love and know Him in the same way that Jesus loves and knows the Father (John 17).

Further, Jesus lived His life dedicated to doing the will of God, an example for us that restores a vision of the goodness of the Father's will. When tempted by Satan to control the course of His life (a repeat of the garden temptation), Christ refused and clung to the word and will of God (Luke 4:1-12). Jesus understood that the Father's will nurtured His own life. It was the food that gave His life meaning and purpose. He trusted it to be good and life-giving (John 4:31-34, 5:30, 6:35-40), leading to His highest destiny and reward (Phil. 2:5-11). He didn't follow God's commands out of duty but out of love, so that the world would have an example to follow (John 14:31).

We will never enter into the fullness of our relationship with God if we continue pridefully operating in our autonomous will. Christ's example gives us hope that we too can learn to trust and love God's will as an extension of our love for Him, allowing us to freely surrender to it. Jesus encourages those who follow Him to exercise faith and believe that immediate circumstances (whether good or bad) are not necessarily indicative of ultimate results. God controls the outcomes in life, and His will promises us abundant life, even when it feels risky to lay down our own strategies for success and survival (Luke 9:23-27).

The good news doesn't stop there, however. Jesus reveals how being restored in relationship with God can also help repair our other relationships as well. Knowing Jesus gives us the hope of knowing ourselves in truth and love. To grow in relationship with God, we not only need to know God in truth, but we need to see ourselves accurately as well. Inadequate knowledge of either person involved in a relationship will stunt the potential for intimacy and love to grow. John Calvin, in his *Institutes of the Christian Religion*, wrote that true wisdom exists in the knowledge of God and the knowledge of self.

During His earthly ministry, Jesus took the time to tell those around Him the truth of their heart condition (Matt. 23). He challenged them to reflect and to care not just about their actions but about the motivations of their hearts (Matt. 5). Jesus practiced a robust form of love, revealing personal truths to people where they were ignorant or deceived, especially it if was inhibiting their relationship with Him (Matt. 16:21-23, John 13:36-38). To abide with Him is to come into the light of all truth, including deeper truth about ourselves.

Lastly, Christ's ongoing ministry to us makes us ministers of reconciliation in our relationships with others as well. Because He loves us, we can love others. Because He shows us grace, we can extend grace to others. Because He forgives us, we can forgive others. Because He has redeemed our lives, we can lay them down for others. We no longer need to compete with others for advantage in light of our scarce personal resources. We can learn how to receive and give freely from the unlimited relational storehouses of our heavenly Father. Because of this reality, we can grow in our ability to be at peace with all men (Rom. 12:9-21).

What better relational news could we hear? This is the gospel, complete in Jesus Christ. He provides a way for us to be reconciled with God, ourselves, and others. Through Him we are invited on a journey that has the hope of renovating our relationships—reversing the devastating consequences of the Fall that plague us all. To Him be the glory forever and ever. Amen.

Pause to Consider

» How familiar are you with these relational aspects of the Gospel of Jesus Christ? Have you personally experienced the Good News as God reconciling us back into relationship with Him, ourselves, and others?

» How might this view of the Gospel affect how you approach your ministry? Your prayer life? Your relationships? Your day-to-day life? Take a few minutes to write down any important thoughts that come to you.

Chapter 5. The Holy Spirit:
The Relational Promise Keeper

"But this is the covenant that I will make with the house of Israel after those days, declares the LORD: I will put my law within them, and I will write it on their hearts. And I will be their God, and they shall be my people. And no longer shall each one teach his neighbor and each brother saying, 'Know the LORD,' for they shall all know me, from the least of them to the greatest, declares the LORD." Jeremiah 31:33-34

Loving God is a characteristic and action that flows from our hearts. We can only fully benefit from Christ's reconciling work when our hearts undergo renovation. We cannot fix our heart problems on our own. We need divine help or, more precisely, a Helper. In a similar way to Adam's need for a suitable helper, we need a Helper perfectly suited to enable our hearts to know God's love and to love Him in return. We need Someone to help us stay relationally connected to the Source of life.

In the last days of Christ's ministry, when He anticipated His physical departure from earth, He informed the disciples that even though He was leaving, they would not be left on their own. He would send the Helper—the One who would teach, remind, reveal truth, and continue to connect the disciples with the essence and words of Christ. He assured His followers that this turn of events was to their advantage (John 16:5-15).

Jesus' promise of the Spirit was meant to comfort the disciples amidst their fear and grief of life without Him. Christ speaks of the Helper's presence as a daily reality—one that His friends would experience, know, and understand in a similar way to His own physical presence with them. The Spirit would be with them forever and would offer them an exclusive relationship (dwelling with and in them) reserved for those who claim Christ, while remaining unseen and unknown by the world at large (John 14:16-17).

On the evening of Resurrection Sunday, Jesus appeared to several of the disciples. After identifying Himself through His crucifixion scars, He breathed on them and told them to receive the Holy Spirit (John 20:19-23). This pointedly symbolic act is especially meaningful in John's gospel. John begins his gospel narrative with the structure of the creation story. He proclaims Christ's presence "In the beginning…" and identifies Jesus as the one through whom all things were made and have life. As the creative force of life, John insinuates that it was the Christ who first breathed life into man in the beginning. Now after His resurrection, He was again breathing on man, this time the Spirit of new life—of spiritual rebirth.

I have to admit, I wonder if that felt like anything. When I read those passages from Scripture I want a tangible relationship. I want to experience life with the Spirit like I experience life with others. I have found that trying to understand how to walk with the Spirit can be mysterious, illusive, frustrating and also unexpectedly miraculous.

The Spirit is integral to the growth of our relationship with God, so let's look at what Scripture says about His ministry in our lives. For those of us in the new covenant of Christ, the indwelling Spirit ministers to our hearts to help us love and know God and to discern His will. His work is perfectly suited to reverse the effects of our spiritual death, awaken us to the possibilities in our relationship with God, and empower us to respond to God's invitations. Scripture reveals that He accomplishes His work in several key ways.

First, He brings us wisdom and helps us understand the true nature of God. The Apostle Paul frequently prayed for the early church that they would be given this ministry of the Spirit. He asks the Father to give a "spirit of wisdom and of revelation in the knowledge of him, having the eyes of your hearts enlightened, that you may know the hope to which he has called you, what are the riches of his glorious inheritance in the saints and what is the immeasurable greatness of his power toward us who believe…" (Eph. 1:16-19).

The knowledge that Paul prays for here is not merely the acquisition of good ideas about God, but an internal heart renovation and acceptance of God's true nature. It is complete buy-in to the incredible goodness of God demonstrated through Christ. Deeply believing these truths compels one to love God in return.

Second, the Spirit testifies to our spirits that we are children of God (Rom. 8:14-17). He renovates our hearts with an awareness of our new identity. It is hard to overstate the relational implications of this incredible ministry of the Spirit. When we deeply accept our adoption as children of God, we are able to cry out to God as our Father. It puts us in the privileged position of heir with Christ and affords us the benefits of His inheritance. This relational reality invites us to engage in a familial way with the Trinity.

Third, the Holy Spirit strengthens our inner man with the love of Christ. In the end, love is the essential transforming ingredient for the human heart and the ground of our relationship with God and others. The Spirit's ministry strengthens and empowers our inner beings to be able to receive, comprehend, and know Christ's dynamic love for us. His work in rooting us in the love of Christ creates a hospitable environment in which Christ can dwell, and also increasingly grows our capacity to be filled with the fullness of God (Eph. 3:14-19).

Becoming filled with God is the process for creating relational intimacy; this is the fulfillment of Christ's priestly prayer in the seventeenth chapter of John: "I do not ask for these only, but also for those who will believe in me through their word, that they may all be one, just as you Father are in me, and I in you, that they may also be in us, so that the world may believe that you have sent me. The glory that you have given me I have given to them, that they may be one even as we are one, I in them and you in me, that they may become perfectly one, so that the world may know that you sent me and loved them even as you loved me" (John 17:20-23).

Fourth, the Spirit understands our heart problems and prays for our weaknesses. We often struggle to know how we should pray for ourselves. The Spirit ministers to us by interceding for us with the Father who perfectly knows the thoughts and intentions of our hearts. Rather than disqualify us, this heart knowledge is something God now uses in His plan to bring us good and to help us conform to the image of Christ. The Spirit's prayers for us are always in line with the will of the Father (Rom. 8:26-28). Even when we cannot pray for God's will, the Spirit within us is praying the will of God for us, humbling us with this incredible gift of grace.

Fifth, the Spirit of Christ helps us to understand His will for us. The Apostle Paul prays for the Colossians that they may be filled with the knowledge of God's will in all spiritual wisdom and understanding (Col. 1:9-14). Paul writes that this knowledge enables us to walk in a manner pleasing to God and to increase in our knowledge of Him. This ministry of the Spirit completes the relational circle of our spiritual lives by enabling us to love God in return. The same Spirit who helps our hearts to comprehend and receive the love of Christ also helps us to engage with that love by participating in the will of God. He empowers us to endure with patient joy, being grateful for the privilege we have to share in the inheritance of Christ. How incredible is that!

Through all of the Holy Spirit's helpful ministries to and for us, He operates as the relational promise keeper in our life with God. He will never leave us alone, and His presence is the guarantee of our ultimate redemption and inheritance (Eph. 1:11-14).

Pause to Consider

» How do you experience the Holy Spirit's activity in your life? Does He feel present and active?

» As you consider the scriptural promises written above regarding the Holy Spirit, which ones do you desire to experience more? Are there any about which you are unsure or skeptical? Take a few minutes to record any thoughts that seem important.

Live Into It

Practice Biblical Literacy

Spend 20 minutes getting to know an Old Testament character that you may not be familiar with. As you read their story, consider what it tells you about God's desire for a loving relationship with us and/or the consequences of a life lived apart from a relationship dependent on God. Notice your reactions towards the character and towards God. Talk with God honestly about what you learn from the story.

Practice Sharing About Jesus

Spend 20 minutes talking to a fellow Christian or family member about your relationship with Jesus. The idea is not to convince the other person of anything, but simply for you to practice focusing on how your relationship with Jesus affects you personally. Notice how easy or difficult this is for you. Talk with God afterwards about your experience.

Practice Walking with the Holy Spirit

Spend 20 minutes praying as you stroll through your neighborhood. As you walk, ask the Holy Spirit to help you notice whatever it is that He wants you to see and to help you pray according to God's will. Notice what is different about this experience of prayer compared to other ways that you tend to pray.

NOTES

DISCUSS TOGETHER

What do you think?

How does the relational nature of the Trinity affect your understanding about how God is involved in your life?

How do you feel?

Do you find it easier to relate to one Person of the Trinity—the Father, the Son or the Holy Spirit—more than another and why?

What about God?

Might God be inviting you to see Him in a new way? Take a moment for everyone to silently talk with God before inviting anyone to share who wants to.

Where to go from here?

What might you want to continue to talk with God about this next week?

NOTES

Week 3

And the Word became flesh and dwelt among us, and we have seen his glory, glory as of the only Son from the Father, full of grace and truth.

For from his fullness we have all received, grace upon grace. For the law was given through Moses; grace and truth came through Jesus Christ.

John 1:14, 16-17

Rest and Receive

Opening Prayer

Find a quiet place to relax where you will not be disturbed by others. Set aside any items which might vie for your attention. Consider God's presence with the following prayer:

Precious Father,

You abide with me daily,
Inviting me to respond in love and dependence.

I want to live in communion with You.
Help me to see where and when I disconnect from
Your presence and grace.

I entrust my days to You.

In the name of Your Son Jesus, Amen.

Scripture Meditations

We have recorded five meditations on the following biblical passages to draw your attention to God throughout the week. Access these recordings at www.graftedlife.org/podcasts (see page 9).

Monday	John 1:14, 16-17
Tuesday	Romans 8:28-29
Wednesday	Ephesians 2:8-10
Thursday	Psalm 139:23-24
Friday	Matthew 7:7-11

Read and Reflect

Chapter 6. The Journey: A Relational Process

Understanding what the Bible teaches about having a relationship with God and about how that relationship contributes to spiritual life sets the stage for transformation. We must, however, move beyond mere acceptance of ideas. We need to engage the concepts in our lives, allowing our relationship with God to affect how we operate day-to-day and relate with others.

Years ago I heard Eugene Peterson speak at a conference. His address focused on Jesus as the Way, the Truth and the Life. One of the points of his talk has stayed with me: We in the church are often very concerned with the Jesus Truth. We want to know it and deliver it to those who are ignorant. But while we are doing that we can forget about the Jesus Way. Jesus is not just the only way to the Father, but there is a texture to the Jesus Way—a way of relating in the world and relating to the Father. Peterson concluded his remarks with this thought: it is only when we combine the Jesus Way with the Jesus Truth that we gain the Jesus life—grow in our ability to live our life the way that He lived His.

Up until that moment, I had not thought deeply about the Jesus Way. In my adult life I had been concerned with the Jesus Truth. I didn't want to be deceived by false doctrine or led astray in my thinking. I carried a sense of vigilance about that. In regard to truth about my conduct, I wanted to understand what God expected of me as a Christian. I paid attention to the behavioral admonitions of Scripture and tried to produce those actions in my life. I worked at it.

But amidst the work were seasons of doubt and reoccurring questions. I would become aware that the list of things that I was trying to obey was actually too long for me to remember. I would get tired of how hard it was to act kind, loving, forgiving, and giving. I served in the church and the world, in part, to quiet the guilt I often took away from Sunday morning sermons. I was earnest, which contributed to a sense that I was never really going to be able to do "enough." When the internal pressure became too intense, I would take a little vacation, a break from God and my spiritual duties until I adequately recouped to get back at it. I used groups of people to keep me accountable, and I secretly wondered if duty and guilt would be my lifelong companions.

I had a way of doing it—a process by which I was living out my Christian life. It wasn't easy, and it often felt burdensome, but it was also the only way I knew. I figured that I was doing my best and I hoped that my best was all that God expected this side of heaven. It wasn't until my spiritual life derailed that I started to consider that my way might not be the Jesus Way.

As I look back, I realize that I had a distorted view of the Jesus Way because I had a shallow view of the Jesus Truth. I placed a high value on knowing things about God—sound doctrines, correct ideas, and behavioral commands. I believed that intellectually knowing these truths would provide me with enough information to live like Jesus. Although I could articulate that I wanted to be changed from the heart, in actuality I was only practicing an externally focused process.

What I now understand is that the Jesus Truth not only encompasses right knowledge about God and the way He has designed our lives to be lived in relationship with Him, but also indispensable truth about humanity—our hearts, our inability to reconnect to God without Jesus, our relational difficulties with others. Discovering these human truths and seeing the dysfunction they can cause in my heart has revolutionized my understanding of the life that Jesus calls me to. The closer I become to Jesus, the more I realize that He is concerned with the postures of my heart: is it humble, loving, willing, and constantly dependent on Him. I have come to experience that when He changes my heart through relationship—my affections, desires, loves, and deep beliefs—the rest of me goes with Him, too. He wins me to His way as a natural end of the process.

Outlining a process of spiritual growth through relationship is a tricky business. There are potential pitfalls right up front. Let me name just a few.

It is easy to sound like you have discovered the Holy Grail or the holy fix for the ills of the church. Solomon wrote that there is nothing new under the sun, and I believe him (Eccles. 1:9). Jesus has successfully been in charge of His church for as long as she has existed. He doesn't need me to fix her. What we are invited to do for each other is to witness. In that spirit, please receive the explanation of this process as a testimony to what Jesus has done in my life and in the lives of those with whom I have journeyed. It has been so life-giving and good, I can't help but share it and desire it for everyone.

An additional pitfall is that it is easy to sound like the process is one-size-fits-all. That idea does injustice to God's creativity and the unique and personal way that He works with His children. In my experience as a spiritual director, I am often amazed at the unusual twists and turns that are a part of people's journeys with God. If Romans 8:28-29 is to be believed, God creatively weaves every individual circumstance in the lives of those who love Him toward the good of conforming them into the image of His Son so that they can become Jesus's siblings. I firmly believe that God has used all the moments of my life to invite me into this family relationship with Him, even the years when I was completely unaware of what He was doing or when I was trying so hard to accomplish personal change in my own strength. One thing everyone's process has in common is that God is in charge of it. Only He knows the way through the heart, including the timing for receptivity to deeper relationship with Him. Only He has the power to strengthen the inner man, to rejuvenate, reconcile and restore.

Lastly, it is hard to articulate a process without turning it into a formula or program. Formulas are just so much easier to explain and quantify. Trying to describe a relationship is hard, especially when the nature of a believer's relationship with God is internal. People can't see the activities in another's soul or what the Spirit may be doing there. As I have gone through this heart journey with God, I have been aware that casual observers might not notice any difference in my life. Circumstantially, things may not look unusual. But internally the landscape has been turned upside down. I can't give you a formula for that. I can offer you wisdom—a way to understand how the truth of Scripture can integrate with real life. I can offer you the explanation of a process that leads you to God and a relationship with Him as the One who knows how to transform your heart into a place where Christ is at home and where He reigns.

Chapter 7. Recognizing the Way of Grace

Paul writes, "For by grace you have been saved through faith. And this is not your own doing; it is the gift of God, not a result of works, so that no one may boast. For we are his workmanship, created in Christ Jesus for good works, which God prepared beforehand, that we would walk in them" (Eph. 2:8-10).

When I started to read and reflect on sanctification and spiritual growth, I was challenged to expand my view of grace. I understood grace as a gift that initially reconciled me with God, but what if grace is also the *means* or *way* of growth? As I pondered that idea it seemed to fit a biblical view. However, I didn't know how to practically live my Christian life with that interpretation of grace. Although I understood that salvation was by grace alone and that I could not work my way to heaven, I lived with a profound sense of responsibility to apply my efforts toward sanctification. I felt I needed to fix the things that I discovered were wrong with me: places where I wasn't conformed to the image of Christ. I didn't know how grace could help me with that. Coming to a relational understanding of the gospel, however, gave me a new perspective on grace.

My sin had made me relationally deficient in a way that only Christ could reconcile. I needed Christ's grace all the time to be connected to God. I wanted to know how to abide in that reality. How could "going to Christ" (Heb. 4:16) become a habit of my heart?

In the spring of 2007 as I was approaching the end of my graduate studies, I had an unexpected invitation from God to practice abiding in my relationship with Him. My husband Curt was offered a job in Dallas, Texas. That doesn't sound all that dramatic unless you understand the context of our lives at that time. We were living in Southern California, in the same house in which we had lived for twenty-two years, where we had raised our kids, and where all three still lived as well.

In addition, through the course of my studies, God had opened my heart to explore what I desired for my life when my kids were grown and on their own. I loved my experience in higher education; I loved my graduate program and the community of people who had journeyed with me through such a season of spiritual awakening. I dreamed of working with them in Southern California in the field of spiritual formation when I graduated. I had recently taken a part-time job at the university and desired to see how that might turn into something more permanent. Moving anywhere was not on my radar screen.

The situation was complicated by the fact that my husband was not fulfilled in the job that he was doing at the time. He and a partner had started a consultancy to non-profits in 2000 and although the business was going well, Curt didn't really enjoy the type of work he was doing. It didn't access his core giftedness or fully leverage his twenty five years of work experience.

During my studies, we had many conversations about what I was learning about God, myself, and the ways we operated together. We became transparent with each other about our internal lives and intentional about including God in those conversations. We shared our hearts as we explored our feelings and desires about our vocations and future. Because we were aware and open to our desires, the offer of the new job carried significant meaning for us. It exposed vulnerable places in both of our souls. For Curt it offered a sense of hope that God may understand and care for him in ways that he had not expected. It was a great job offer that seemed to fit what he was longing for in ways beyond our wildest dreams. For me it seemed a place of grief, of unfulfilled longing and disappointment. It would require that I let go of many things.

As you can imagine, we were at a bit of an impasse. How could we both get what we desired? As we were navigating our way through the process of making a decision about the job, we went to dinner one night and had a revealing conversation. Curt had gone to lunch with a friend that day who challenged him to think about his role as my husband. He asked Curt what it would look like to give his life sacrificially for me like Christ gave His life for the church. As we were sitting at dinner, just the two of us, Curt told me about his lunch and then said that he was not going to take the job in Dallas. He wanted me to have the opportunity to live my dreams and stay in California and work.

Almost immediately, I felt a strong emotional reaction to Curt's words. I couldn't talk and I started to cry. I wasn't experiencing relief or even gratitude although I recognized that his offer was loving and sincere. I couldn't eat anymore of my dinner and we left the restaurant. As we drove, I struggled to understand and articulate what I was feeling. Through choking sobs, I finally got out that I could not let him do that. I explained that deep in my heart was the belief that it was my job to give my life to make others' lives fulfilled, whether that was him, the kids, or other family members and friends. As those words hung in the air, I heard a still, small voice within me state, "No, it was my job to give My life and I have already done it."

Curt and I were at a crossroad in our life, but it wasn't so much about whether we would live in Texas or California; rather it was about how we would live with God in either of those places. Would we stumble over ourselves, trying to fix it for each other, or would we risk opening our hearts and desires to a journey with a Savior who had already given His life for us? Could we take this issue to Christ to find mercy and grace?[1]

The truth is that we all need a Savior. We need a Savior not only to forgive our sins but also to free us from the sinful habits that are rooted in our hearts. We need a transforming Savior every day of our lives. We need Him every moment of our lives. No matter where we are in our spiritual journey, that fact never changes. So how can we live in light of that truth? How can we function in a life of grace?

I think the first step toward experiencing the way of grace is to humble our hearts with the truth of our weaknesses and needs. Saying that we need a Savior and feeling the actual struggles and needs in our lives can be two different things. Some of us are uncomfortable when confronted with our weakness. Recognizing our needs, however, is important. God loves to help us discover our needs and loves when we admit them (Luke 18:9-14). He desires that we know our hearts honestly and look to Him for help (Heb. 4:11-16).[2]

---

1   In offering this illustration, I feel it wise to make a clarification. I do believe that there are times in our lives when Jesus asks us to give sacrificially to others whether that is our time, our money, the postponement of our dreams, etc. Giving in this way is a part of loving in the way that Jesus loves. In the particular situation that Curt and I faced, God was free to ask us to give to each other in that way, but until we opened our hearts to having our needs met by Jesus, we would not know that for sure. Until we allowed God to search our hearts and our motives by turning to Him in relationship, we were in danger of hurting ourselves and each other through devising and carrying out our own plans.

2   During the course of this section on the process of relationship, I am assuming that the reader accepts that our emotions—the way we feel about things—are important and that we should pay attention to them in our relationships with God and others. I realize that people may struggle to identify the emotions that they feel. Some believers become defensive when emotions become the topic of conversation, preferring to instead focus on facts and ideas. I have found in my life and in my work with others that it is impossible to open up our hearts before God without dealing with our emotions. Expressing our feelings often helps to clear

As Curt and I sat in our car that night, others might have admired us as a loving couple, willing to sacrificially give up personal dreams and aspirations for the other. To some extent we were willingly sacrificial. But there was a deeper truth. Our needs were exposed, and they spilled out all over the car. Curt needed answers to his questions about God's love and care for him and how God may be using his unrest in his job to unveil his heart in this area. I clearly had a distorted view of my role in life and needed to believe that Jesus's death had secured a future for me that I was unable to earn by my actions, no matter how "sacrificial." We couldn't fix these needs for each other. We could only recognize them together.

In order for any of us to recognize our needs and struggles in life, we have to pay attention to the way we are feeling. Our emotions can be first indicators to deep issues in our hearts. The following possible scenarios illustrate this principle:

» I get angry with my wife when she does (fill in the blank). In fact, I may have a problem with anger.

» I feel insecure about God's love for me. I often feel like a disappointment.

» I hate my job. I feel discouraged and undervalued. I wish I could find work that was better suited to my talents.

» I am worried and afraid that I won't be able to provide for my family through a season of unemployment.

---

the way for God to help us understand our hearts. Conversely, not expressing or denying our feelings can "congest" our hearts—cause us to be stuck in unresolved places, make it hard to understand ourselves, hear God in truth, respond to Him in freedom.

If you or someone you know is struggling to believe that their emotions are important, I suggest a reflective read through the Psalms. These ancient songs encourage us that God invites His people to recognize and express the full range of their emotions to Him.

» I am single and lonely.

» I am frustrated or feel guilty about my inability to get control of my behavior (insert your particular attachment/addiction here: food, sex, pornography, gambling, shopping, achievements, etc.).

» I am supposed to love the people in my church but there is a woman in my Bible study that really bugs me.

» I have a chronic physical ailment. I am in physical pain. I am angry or disappointed that God hasn't healed me.

» I am supposed to forgive, but I feel resentment about things that happened to me in my past.

Acknowledging our feelings can help us to articulate our struggles. Whatever the nature of the need, whether physical, mental, spiritual or emotional, God wants us to admit it. Every need can be brought into our relationship with Him.

Once we recognize that we have a need, we can then allow space for God to help us see that need more clearly. We can be present with our need and God. I know that sounds a little esoteric, but bear with me because I have found this to be an important part of the process. Often when we become aware of a need, we go into autopilot. We engage in some instinctive behavior to deal with it. Some of us just put the struggle out of our minds because we don't like the feelings that emerge when we become aware of it. Our awareness of needs may bring up anxiety, fear, anger, disappointment, or other unpleasant emotions that we don't want to feel. Others of us try to dispense with the need in our own strength by quickly devising a plan for taking care of it. This is what Curt and I were tempted to do in the car that night. Still others of us latch onto our struggles, using them as a whip to beat ourselves up. Somehow by feeling bad about ourselves, we feel better.

If, however, we can learn to push the pause button on our re-action to the awareness of a struggle or need, we can allow God to invite us into a new opportunity in our relationship with Him. I have come to believe that God constantly invites us to see the truth of our hearts because on our own we are prone to see ourselves incorrectly. His invitation to view our hearts realistically is a great benefit of relating with Jesus, who is the Truth, and with the Spirit, who dwells in our hearts. We can take the time to prayerfully reflect on the state of our hearts. When we become aware of struggles and needs, we can ask God to help us discover what is really going on internally (Ps. 139:23-24). Some possible questions to take into prayer might be:

» LORD, have You made me aware of this need for a reason? Is there something more You want to show me?

» What am I feeling in the midst of this struggle? Are there emotions that You would like for me to pay attention to or talk with You about?

» Is this my true need or is it masking something deeper?

» Has this struggle revealed beliefs about myself or You that You would like to correct?

This prayerful conversation and posture of listening could take an afternoon, several days, or reoccur for many months. It could happen one-on-one with God or through additional dialogue with a trusted confidant who helps us to see ourselves truthfully. In Curt and my Dallas dilemma, the process happened over time through our conversations as we were willing to be honest with each other and God about our feelings, hopes, fears, and dreams about the future. The main point is that truthfully acknowledging our struggles and needs starts a process of grace in our lives, one which invites us to intentionally engage in our relationship with God.

The second step toward experiencing the way of grace involves humbling our hearts by asking for God's help. When God invites us into a life of grace, He requires us to acknowledge that we cannot meet our needs, fix our hearts, conquer our struggles, etc. on our own. We need His help; we need His wisdom and His plan. We simply need Him to rescue us. That is the essence of grace.

One of the heart tendencies we bring into our relationship with God is our fallen habit of autonomy—our practice of operating on our own, independently from God and often from others as well. We try to figure out our own lives, depending on our wisdom to find solutions. To amplify our autonomous pattern, we are influenced by societal values of success, competency, and independence. Consequently many of us become uncomfortable when we need to ask for help.

Asking for help humbles our hearts yet more deeply than accepting the truth of our needs does. Asking for help makes our needs feel more real. It is like saying something out loud that you have been thinking in your head. Asking for help requires that we act on the idea that God created us to be dependent on a relationship with Him.

As I look back on that important time in Curt's and my life, I realize in parts of our hearts, we were seeking God and His will for us. But because it was an emotionally stressful situation, God was also revealing other areas of our hearts—places where we still operated in instinctively autonomous ways. When pressed, those heart habits came to the surface causing us to believe that there were only two possible solutions to our dilemma: Curt would give up his dream or I would give up mine. It took awhile for us to recognize that maybe Jesus had another plan. We needed to ask Him about that. Might He be planning to give us both what we were longing for in a way yet unrevealed? Did we have the faith to ask Him to meet both of our needs through His grace?

Jesus instructs us to ask for the things we need (Matt. 7:7-11, Luke 11:1-13). The act of asking invites us to a new level of involvement in our relationship with Him. It vulnerably opens our hearts before Him and can uncover dynamics that God would like to bring to our attention.

Asking for help can reveal places where we struggle in our relationship with God and with others, as well. We may discover ways in which we distrust God, and doubt His love for us, His care for our needs, or His willingness to help our situation. We might need to talk often with God about our fears, our disappointments, and our unworthy beliefs about who He is.

We could also discover that other relationships are influencing our relationship with God. If we have been wounded by others who have broken our trust, we may find it difficult to ask for help, even from God. We might need to process and understand these past hurts in order to risk engaging with God in this way.

Asking for help might be a long process. It could require a season of endurance where our requests are refined. We may struggle to understand and articulate what we are asking for. We will likely need for our faith to expand as we wait for God to respond.

Asking also invites us to become more attuned to the ways that God is answering our requests—in other words, to grow in our knowledge and experience of Him. God can offer us comfort or a deeper awareness of His love for us. He could provide a job or other tangible gifts to supply physical needs. God may bring others into our lives to meet our needs or even to help us through the process. He might direct us to support groups, recovery groups, counselors, or other helping ministries who invite us into community and offer tangible help. God may reveal to us that part of His plan of provision requires us to ask for help from others in the body of Christ.

As Curt and I opened our hearts before God regarding the job offer in Dallas, we were invited into a season of asking. As we talked and prayed together, we discerned that Curt should take the job in Dallas and we should prepare to move. We felt that God was not asking us to sacrifice for each other in this situation, but rather to believe that, although we could only see part of the plan at the moment, in His timing He would provide for both of our vocational needs. We knew this was something only God could do. Our dreams and plans were insufficient.

I don't want to paint some rosy picture of that time in my life. Remaining in a posture of asking for my vocational needs was a painfully hard process and lasted about two years. As I suspected, there were many things I had to grieve and let go of in my life, not the least of which was my personal vision for my future. That happens sometimes. But humbling my heart through those years and continuing to ask God to provide for me also encouraged me to grab onto some essential things my heart needed. The process brought me consistently back to my relationship with God, it deepened my prayer life, it kept exposing areas of my heart that doubted, and over time it strengthened my capacity to trust and hold on to God.

No matter the duration or texture of a particular season of asking, God is gracious to deepen our relationship with Him through the process. Asking is a relational activity. It requires us to show up, to engage, possibly to abandon our hearts to the possibilities of a life fully invested with God.

In the third step toward experiencing the way of grace, we humble our hearts by receiving what God provides. In the last couple years I have done a lot of thinking about what it means to be a receiver. I've observed over and again the difficulty that many of us have in regard to receiving provisions in our lives. Receiving the gracious gifts of God humbles our hearts by confirming the reality that we cannot earn or work for these gifts. We don't deserve them and yet they are ours for the taking.

When I reflect on the act of receiving, it seems as if it should be simple and even a joyous part of our Christian experience. Who wouldn't like to receive a free gift? I doubt many people would turn down lottery winnings or the grand prize of a sweepstakes. These lucky occurrences don't seem to require humility in order to receive. The random, unexpected nature of them makes them impersonal.

Receiving God's provision after asking for help, however, is deeply personal. It is an act of relational intimacy; it assumes that God sees us for who we really are and knows what we need, maybe in ways we don't realize. It is a glorious and potentially frightening proposition. We desperately want it and might also fear it at the same time. In receiving from God, we must exercise our humble belief that He knows best and has our good at heart.

Personally, I have struggled mightily with this step into the life of grace. There are many competing realities in my heart. I want to be known by God, but what if He gives me something that I wasn't expecting? What if His gift allows me to feel misunderstood about the thing I requested? I don't want to feel misunderstood in my relationship with Him. I don't want to be disappointed, and because of that, I don't want to give up control. I don't want to be surprised by what God asks me to receive.

You can see how receiving from God drives us deeper into the realities of our hearts and exposes places where we still operate in self-motivated or protective ways. We may experience strong emotional responses, such as:

» I feel guilty because I don't deserve to receive anything from God.

» I feel too exposed or too much shame for God to see me this clearly.

» If I take this gift, what will God expect from me? What will I be obligated to pay in return?

» What if taking this gift will expose other emotions that I don't want to feel, places where I have been hurt by others who have not loved me well?

» I don't even understand the "provision." It seems as if God is answering my pleas by sending me to someone else for help.

Can't He just heal/fix me? I don't want to have to expose my problems to another person or group.

» Why is God helping me now? There were other times in my life when I could have used His help, and He wasn't there.

The intimacy of receiving puts us face to face with God and our real self. It exposes places in our relationship where we would rather keep God on the periphery and handle things on our own. It drives us deeper into humility and invites us to know God experientially as our provider.

About a year after Curt and I arrived in Dallas, I began to see a vision for how God was providing vocational work for me. It didn't circumstantially fit any of my previous ideas. In fact, it would require that we start a new nonprofit. I had never thought about doing something that adventurous before. I wasn't sure I wanted to. Over time it became clear, though, that this work was a gift God was asking me to receive; it was the answer to my prayers.

Receiving this gift from God has been amazing and much harder than I anticipated. It has required me to develop perseverance. I asked Curt repeatedly throughout the start-up process, "When you get your 'dream job' is it normal to want to quit about every other week?" The work has asked more of me than I thought I had to give. It has stretched, pushed, and prodded me into an awareness of my utter dependence on God. It has revealed to me how deeply God knows and sees me—the needs of my heart, places where He is restoring, refining, and healing and also places where He is providing fulfillment, fellowship, and enjoyment beyond my hopes. It is like living in the best and most effective hospital and the most enjoyable playground at the same time! I would never have been able to pull that off on my own. That is a provision that only God could graciously give.

In one sense, receiving completes our heart posture of humility and brings us full circle in our life of grace—recognizing our needs, asking for God's help, and then fully receiving God's provision. In another equally real sense, it causes us to want more, to open up to new needs, and to start the process again. I love how this truth is expressed in Psalm 118. In this song, the psalmist talks specifically about how Israel went through this process of humility. They were in need, they cried out to the LORD for help, and He saved them. The psalmist sees God's provision as an expression of His goodness and steadfast love. In verses 23-24 he leads the people to recognize that only God could do this. This day of salvation was a day they owed to God; it was His doing, He made it possible. The writer calls for a response of praise and rejoicing.

Then in verse 25 he writes something unexpected. "Save us, we pray, O LORD! Oh LORD, we pray, give us success!" Receiving from God seems to have emboldened him to ask for more—to realize that living dependently with God was good and right. This Psalm demonstrates that this process of humility is not just a foxhole remedy—the answer for getting out of a particular jam. It is meant to be a way of life—a repeating pattern in the heart of a follower of Christ. As we journey in this way of grace, humbling our hearts to recognize our need, to ask for God's help, and to receive His provision, may we too be moved to joyfully cry out, "Save us again, O LORD! We need your grace!"

PAUSE TO CONSIDER

» How often do you respond to the hurdles of life in this rhythm of grace—continually humbling your heart through these three movements: recognizing your need, asking for help, receiving from God?

» When you reflect on your own experience, is one of the movements more difficult for you than the others? What factors might contribute to that?

» Is there a need surfacing in your life right now? What might it look like to move through these three steps with God regarding that need? Spend some time talking with God about your need, and then write down a few sentences that describe your prayer experience.

LIVE INTO IT

Practice Acknowledging Your Need

Spend 20 minutes talking to God about a need that you currently have in your life. If you're not sure what that could be, ask the Holy Spirit to help reveal it to you. Talk with God about the circumstances around this need, your feelings about it, and your history with it. Note how this experience of prayer is similar or different to how you usually pray.

Practice Asking for Help

Spend 20 minutes asking God for help with some particular need or circumstance in your life. Explore several different ways that you would like God to help you. Notice if you are more or less attached to particular ways that God could answer your request. Talk to God about how you would feel if He helped you in ways different from what you want.

Practice Receiving from God

Spend 20 minutes making a list of things that you have received from God this week. Include both things directly from Him and things that God might have provided through other people. Note how easy or difficult it is for you to write this list. Notice how writing this list makes you feel towards God.

NOTES

DISCUSS TOGETHER

What do you think?

What do you think about this process of grace that involves recognizing your need, asking for help and receiving from God? How is this similar or different to how you normally relate to God?

How do you feel?

Which aspect of this rhythm of grace feels the easiest for you? Which feels the most difficult?

What about God?

Is there something that God wants you to bring to Him right now? Allow everyone some time for personal private prayer, then let anyone share who feels led to.

Where to go from here?

If you have not yet tried one of the Week 3 Live Into It activities, is there one that you might want to engage with this week?

NOTES

Week 4

As the Father has loved me, so have I loved you. Abide in my love. If you keep my commandments, you will abide in my love, just as I have kept my Father's commandments and abide in his love. These things I have spoken to you, that my joy may be in you, and that your joy may be full.

This is my commandment, that you love one another as I have loved you. Greater love has no one than this, that someone lay down his life for his friends. You are my friends if you do what I command you. No longer do I call you servants, for the servant does not know what his master is doing; but I have called you friends, for all that I have heard from my Father I have made known to you.

You did not choose me, but I chose you and appointed you that you should go and bear fruit and that your fruit should abide, so that whatever you ask the Father in my name, he may give it to you. These things I command you, so that you will love one another.

John 15:9-17

Rest and Receive

Opening Prayer

Find a quiet place to relax where you will not be disturbed by others. Set aside any items which might vie for your attention. Consider God's presence with the following prayer:

Reigning Lord,

You lead my life in this present moment.
I want to always follow You.

Teach me Your ways,
Sensitize my heart to the movements of Your Spirit.
Guide me through the community of Your saints.
I commit my way to You.

In the name of my Shepherd, Jesus, Amen.

Scripture Meditations

We have recorded five meditations on the following biblical passages to draw your attention to God throughout the week. Access these recordings at www.graftedlife.org/podcasts (see page 9).

Monday	John 15:9-17
Tuesday	Romans 5:1-5
Wednesday	Hebrews 4:12-13
Thursday	Colossians 3:12-15
Friday	Ephesians 3:14-21

READ AND REFLECT

Chapter 8. Participating in Relationship

A friend of mine recently took in a seventeen-year-old exchange student. The boy was transferring from another home where he was unhappy. My friend had hosted exchange students in the past, some of whom became her lasting friends. After praying and talking it over, her family was excited about the opportunity to invite this boy to live with them through the rest of the school year.

Within forty-eight hours of the boy's arrival, the reality of the situation dashed their expectations. Their guest refused to communicate. When they weren't providing a meal for him, he stayed in his room with the door closed. He asked no questions. He said no words except to answer a direct question. If nothing changed, they had little opportunity for relationship with their guest, despite his presence in their home.

The participation of both parties is fundamental to any relationship's success. For instance, we can rationally understand that we are related to our ancestors, but if they died before we were born, we didn't participate with them in relationship. We didn't know them personally. In the same way, we can mentally grasp that we are adopted into the family of God, but unless we engage with God, we can't enjoy that relationship—we can't know God and feel known by Him. Like my friend's exchange student, unless we come out of isolation and participate in life together, there is little opportunity to experience relationship, no matter how close the physical proximity.

So how can we participate in our relationship with God?

In some ways our relationship with God is similar to our other relationships in life. We need to give it our time and attention. We can communicate, do activities (whether work or leisure) together, share our hearts, be honest with each other, give to one another, and over time build affection and trust. In light of our relational brokenness, however, we also need to recognize the difficulties we can face when we attempt to relate with God. We can discover places in our hearts where we are tempted to hide, evade the truth, deceive ourselves, believe we are unlovable, blame others for our difficulties, and find it hard to trust. Facing these realities can feel scary. If we are honest, thinking about getting close to God—giving Him our full attention and feeling His attention on us—may be the very thing we are trying to avoid.

When I applied for entrance into my seminary program, part of the requirement was a personal interview. I remember my experience that day as I sat and talked with two professors who I would potentially be "apprenticing" with for the next three years. They asked serious questions about why I desired to attend the program, about me as a person, about my spiritual journey, and about my family's thoughts regarding my enrollment at that time. I can't remember very many details about the answers to those questions, but I vividly recall what I felt as I walked away from our conversation. I felt exposed.

Somehow I knew they were able to see more of me than I was purposefully presenting in the room. It dawned on me that maybe they were able to see things about me I didn't even know about myself, didn't want to admit, or didn't desire for them to see. I was confronted with questions of my own in the next few days. Did I want to give up feeling like I was in control of my image to participate in this program and to have a relationship with them? Did I need to understand what they saw in my life? Could I handle the feelings of fear that came with exposure? Did they have my good at heart? Could I trust them?

When we think about participating in a relationship with God, similar feelings and questions may emerge. Even if we can rationally and theologically answer all of these questions in affirming ways, our hearts can still feel at risk. For some of us, we might not be able to move forward until we look honestly at these feelings.

Admitting and exploring fearful emotions will likely be the place where we need to begin to talk with God.

As we evaluate participating in our relationship with God, it is also important to think about how our relationship with Him is different from our relationships with everyone and everything else we know. He is unique, and He offers us relationship in unique ways. Some of these ways are comforting, whereas others are quite challenging.

One such unique challenge is that God relates to us through the physical and also transcends the physical.

There are many ways that we can relate to God through physical realities. One primary gift is our physical Bible: words of inspired and inerrant revelation in a book. Scripture privileges us to hear about God, to reflect on who He reveals Himself to be and how He has invited us to be reconciled to Him. The word of God is an endless source of relational invitations from Him to know Him and ourselves in truth. It helps us to learn what it means to be loved by God, to love Him and others, and to recognize how we don't love. We can engage with Scripture by listening, reading, meditating, memorizing etc. with the intent to allow God to instruct us and expose whatever is useful and necessary for Him in working with our hearts and in calling us into relationship with Himself (Heb. 4:12-13, 2 Tim. 3:16-17).

We can also recognize His work and involvement in the physical creation of our world, and respond in humility, praise, and worship. That He provides us with food, shelter, work etc. can help us experience His deep love and care for us. We can show our love in return by offering expressions of gratitude.

In addition, we can meditate on the love that God shows us through sending His Son as a man to live among us, to die for us, and to conquer death through His resurrection. We can receive the comfort which God's love offers us—to know that Jesus completely understands and has faced the experiences and temptations that we face as human beings in a fallen world, yet without sin. We can act on this knowledge by bringing our problems to Him, asking for His help and receiving His grace and mercy (Eph. 3:14-19, Heb. 4:14-16).

Lastly, we can see God's activity in our circumstances—how He uses trials to make us aware of our needs, to help us see that we have limited control in life, and to encourage us to depend on Him (Rom. 5:1-5, Jas. 1:2-5). We can respond by looking for the ways that God is inviting us into relationship through the events of our days and to prayerfully ask Him, "How are You involved in these events of my life? What do You want to show me? How are You calling me to be with You through these circumstances?" We can then listen for how God might answer those questions.

It might be easy to see how God is present in these physical ways in our life, but He also transcends the physical. He is not confined by the physical things we can see or touch.

God exists in Spirit and invites us into relationship in the spiritual realities of life as well.

Even though we too have a spirit as a part of our person, this aspect of our lives may be hard for us to understand. In turn, we could find it difficult to know how to engage with Him. We can experience this struggle for several reasons.

God is not limited by space or time. As believers, we cannot be separated from God. This is a unique quality in our relationship with Him. We can experience separation in every other relationship we have on earth, either by choice or through circumstances. We cannot, however, be apart from God, even if we try to flee (Ps. 139, Rom. 8:38-39). We take God with us everywhere, in everything we do. He is always present with us. This relational reality has the potential to comfort us, irritate us, frighten us, or leave us with a mix of emotions. It can be a grand invitation or a huge stumbling block. We might discover that we wish we could escape God's notice. Conversely we could be longing to know the presence of God but feel that the experience of His presence has always eluded us. Despite our best efforts and prayers, we may still feel alone.

God has chosen to abide within us. He has sent the Holy Spirit to live within the heart of believers (Rom. 8:9-11, 1 Cor. 3:16).

Again this is completely unique to the spiritual capacities of God and unlike any of our other relationships.

Earlier I mentioned the interview I had with my professors in graduate school. That experience helped me realize that relating with them would offer me the opportunity to receive their feedback about my life. If I was willing to listen, their observations could help me to understand myself more deeply and discover things about myself that I didn't know. In spite of their experience and maturity, though, I still had the capacity to hide the "real" me from them. Our physical separation as human beings inhibited their ability to fully read my mind, or completely see my heart. I remained in some control of the level of intimacy. This position of power is true of all of our earthly relationships.

We are not in control, however, in our relationship with God. Even though God does not have to send His Spirit to live within us in order to completely know the condition of our hearts, He purposefully does send Him to live within believers (John 14:25-26, 15:26, 16:5-15). When we ponder this relational reality we conclude that we don't have the power to manage the level of intimacy that we offer to God. We are fully known by Him— God comprehends each emotion, motivation, thought, desire, and attachment of our hearts and minds. He lives amidst the reality of our internal world (Rom. 8:26-27). He occupies the places where we are hiding from ourselves and others.

Read that last line again. You might want to pause right here for a few minutes to let that concept sink in and explore how your heart responds to it.

From our perspective, given this spiritual reality, what possible subject could be off limits in our conversations with God? We can talk with Him about anything and everything—all of our feelings and thoughts, our confusions and anxieties. We can ask God to help us understand ourselves and reveal to us the true condition of our hearts (Ps. 139:23-24). We can learn the joy of abiding communication (prayer without ceasing—1 Thess. 5:17) because we have no need to hide from His presence. We can spend time just giving our attention to God, without words, resting in the truth that He knows us intimately and we have no need to defend or explain ourselves. We can receive and enjoy God's love for us.

From the Spirit's perspective, this reality also allows Him to bring problem areas in our hearts to our attention—to start conversations with us (John 16:13). What I have come to believe over time is that when I feel emotions surface in my heart, especially if they are discouraging me from engaging with God, then the Spirit has probably brought that reality of my heart to my attention. Is this a relational invitation from God to talk over those feelings with Him, to ask Him to help me understand the source of that emotion, to find its meaning? Since the Spirit is living within us, it makes sense that He uses the conditions of our internal world (our thoughts, emotions, reactions) to get our attention, in a similar way that He uses the external circumstances of our lives.

In our life of grace, we are meant to bring our troubles to Christ to receive His mercy and grace, rather than attempting to fix our problems in our own strength. This may be especially true regarding the often tangled condition of our hearts. The Spirit's vantage point within assures us that He knows what needs to be addressed: our hidden hurts, our resentments, the harmful beliefs and motivations that lead us to the same sins time and again. He sees where we need to heal, forgive and trust, where we need to feel the love of God so that we can relinquish our lesser loves. He knows the plan to write truth on our hearts (Jer. 31:33, Heb. 8:10).

What might it look like to participate in relationship with the Spirit as He actively intercedes and works in our hearts? We can start by paying attention to our internal world. We could set aside time each day to reflect on our reactions to the day, to identify our feelings, express them to God and ask Him about their significance. As we submit our hearts to the Holy Spirit, we trust Him to bring whatever is helpful to our minds and then take the journey of grace with Him wherever that may lead. Our interactions with the Bible are particularly helpful with this process of opening our hearts before the Spirit. The word of God can cut open the heart and expose the thoughts and intentions deeply buried beneath the surface. We can then intentionally talk with Christ about what is brought to our attention (Heb. 4:12-16).

It has been about eight years since I first started praying in this way—intentionally spending time with God to explore my internal life before Him and talk over whatever seemed pressing on my heart. It started as a formal exercise, with specific issues in mind, but the focus was to spend time with God and to invite Him into a reflection of my life. We have included reflective questions through this book to invite you to experience this type of prayer.

I will admit that getting used to praying in this way was a challenge. I wasn't accustomed to learning so much about myself. My capacity to talk with God about my internal life was limited. My mind wandered away from prayer and the subject matter constantly. I didn't know how to recognize God talking to me or know how to distinguish His voice from my own thoughts. I instinctively wanted to fix everything "bad" that I discovered because it made me so uncomfortable. And to further complicate things, I was often afraid of what God might reveal to me about myself. It was like praying with one spiritual eye shut in hopes of blurring what I might see.

It took time to get comfortable with this ministry of the Holy Spirit, to trust that God wasn't out to condemn me, to learn to ask for His love in places where I felt unlovable. I was a little overwhelmed at times by what came out of my heart and into my awareness through the process—things that I felt and believed but I had no idea were there. I began to trust that when I discovered the reality of my heart, God was involved in the process. Although it was painful at times, it was also freeing. I began to experience how the truth can free a person, can lift the burden of hiding and open up opportunities for love, growth, and a genuine desire for obedience. Until I started to feel that freedom, I didn't know how trapped I was by the unexplored terrain of my heart.[1]

If we are willing to take the risk, we can practice and grow in our capacity to dialogue with God about our internal world. We can do this without condemnation because we are clothed in Christ and because He already knows everything that is there (Rom. 8:1-11). He longs for us to abide with Him in truth, to surrender the whole

---

1 Whenever we engage in experiences of listening prayer, where we expect or invite the LORD to speak or reveal truth to us, it is wise to keep practices of discernment in place. When I speak of "revealing truth," I am not referring to instances of special or extra-biblical revelation. I believe the canon of Scripture is closed and complete. I am referring to the process of how God applies truth to our hearts, how He grows us relationally as His children and how He makes us aware of internal areas of sin in our thoughts, beliefs, and feelings. This understanding also extends to discerning God's will for us personally, again not with the liberty of contradicting His expressed will in Scripture, but in illuminating what it looks like to personally follow Him daily, the nuances of loving Him and others in a Christ honoring way. In the same sense that Christ was dependent on doing the will of the Father, we are dependent on doing the will of the Father. The Holy Spirit has been sent to help us know how that truth applies specifically in our circumstances.

Listening for God's voice can be done in a discerning fashion. It is a spiritual privilege of our relationship with God that we should engage in responsibly. It is best to include good study of the Bible in the process, as well as the feedback of scripturally sound, wise, and experienced members of the Body of Christ. Seeking discernment is an activity that is done in community as we submit ourselves to the unity of the Spirit that can come from the Body praying and seeking the LORD together while submitting our lives to the Word. As we participate in this way, overtime we attune our hearts to the aroma and texture of the LORD's movements, building our spiritual capacities to understand what the LORD may be trying to reveal. We learn to recognize truth in our inner being as the Spirit confirms it on our hearts and the hearts of those journeying with us who also seek, love, and serve Jesus.

There are particular, one-another ministries that can also help us to grow in discernment. Spiritual direction, either in a one-on-one setting or in a group, is designed to partner individuals as they are seeking to recognize where God is working in their lives in order to follow Christ more closely. Christian counseling or therapy can also help to uncover emotions, thoughts, or beliefs that are hindering our relationship with God, especially if those heart issues stem from relational hurts from our past.

of our hearts to Him in love. As we journey with Him through the reality of our hearts, we have many opportunities to see the areas where we still resist His love, lack faith, take care of ourselves, and need Him to help us with our unbelief. Along the way He also reveals where He has inspired love for Him, ourselves, and others; where He has confirmed truth, loved us, healed, comforted, and fashioned us closer to the image of Jesus. Because He lives within, He is always inviting us to a process of deepening heart discovery, refinement, and renovation.

When we reflect on all the different ways that God invites us to participate with Him in relationship—through the physical and in the spiritual—we realize that there are opportunities all around us and within us to connect with God. Sadly, one of the main consequences of sin is that it isolates us from the very relationship that we need and for which we are deeply longing. Like the international student who came to live with my friend, we may figuratively be hiding in our rooms, afraid or reluctant to come out and participate in the relationship that God is offering to us.

If that is true, there is still good news. Even in our secret dens we are not alone. The Spirit is present and ready to begin to engage with us in the darkest and smallest of hiding places. We need only open our hearts with the willingness to participate, and He will lead us from there.

PAUSE TO CONSIDER

» What are some of the primary ways that you tend to experience your relationship with God? Are there other ways listed in this chapter that you haven't experienced, but that intrigue you?

» Have you ever brought the "reality of your heart" into communication with the Holy Spirit? How do you feel about the idea of attending to your internal world and sharing what you find there with God?

» What do you tend to do when you discover something "bad" about yourself? Do you tend to ignore it, try and fix yourself, or make quick apologies? What might it be like to simply bring these uncomfortable aspects of yourself into an honest and open conversation with God? Take a moment to talk with God about this and jot down what you learn.

Chapter 9. Participating with God in Community

"Finally, brothers, rejoice. Aim for restoration, comfort one another, agree with one another, live in peace, and the God of love and peace will be with you." 2 Corinthians 13:11

In the previous chapter we explored in depth how it can look to participate with God in an intimate, individual relationship. Often it is difficult to grasp or engage in these relational activities, simply because God is a Spirit. It can feel like we are talking to the air or just ourselves, that our prayers are hitting the ceiling and bouncing back to fall on our ears alone. We may read in the Bible about Jesus's earthly life and long to be able to talk with Him like the apostles did, to have an actual meal with Him, to see the expression on His face or experience His physical embrace of comfort. Our struggle to attune our spiritual senses to "see and hear" the Spirit of God might leave us feeling like there is something wrong with us or that we are somehow disqualified from the experiences that other Christians report. We may well find ourselves feeling isolated and alone.

There is another unique aspect to our relationship with God, however, that addresses our needs in this area. When we are reconciled to God through Christ, not only do we receive the gift of the indwelling Spirit as our companion and guide, but we are also placed within a new family of people. We become part of the body of believers that represents not only the spiritual, but the physical presence of Christ. The Holy Spirit who dwells in us also dwells among us when we meet together (Matt. 18:20). Because this community represents the Body of Christ, engaging with them in relationship is one way we participate in our relationship with God. It is also a part of our spiritual growth. We are changed through the work of the indwelling Holy Spirit on our hearts, as well as through His work in our interactions as a body (Eph. 3:14-19, Eph. 4:1-16). Understanding a little about how the Holy Spirit might use other believers for our growth can be helpful.

First, we need to keep in mind that we are entering into relationship with other believers through our relationship with Christ. We are not meant to figure out by ourselves how to get along together, essentially practicing communal autonomy. God intends us to look to Christ together to learn how we are to get along, love, encourage, and grow with one another. Jesus supplies the grace when we collectively put our faith in Him as our mediator and LORD. He is our common bond, the reason for our relationship to one another. He sets our agenda as our Head. He unifies us as we grow in our ability to look to Him while abiding in communal dependence (Eph. 2:11-22).

Second, entering into relationship with God through the body of believers is often a messy process. When each of us engages in relationship with God, one of the participants in the relationship—God—is not relationally broken. When we engage with God together as a body of believers, the number of relationally broken participants multiplies! This is actually a great good for us, but hard to navigate at times and makes it inevitable that we will wound each other along the way. That fact may sound harsh, but it is real. In spite of this truth, God instructs us to be on the journey toward full relational restoration—to love Him and our neighbor as ourselves. To learn how to love others through Him, we need to practice with someone. He has asked Christians to practice on each other in community (John 13:34-35).

Third, we need to give and receive the unique gifts that the Spirit has supplied to each of us in the body. We can receive teaching, encouragement, practical help, hospitality, discernment, wisdom, mercy, healing etc. from others as we abide in Christ together. In return we offer gifts, depending on our personal giftedness from the Spirit, to others in Jesus's name (1 Cor. 12).

When we engage with each other in this way, the Spirit invites us to humble our hearts by receiving Christ's help through the means He has ordained. This invitation to humility is particularly poignant when we give gifts with an awareness of our brokenness and receive them gratefully from equally broken people. Understanding our collective brokenness encourages us toward greater dependence on Christ as a community as well as in our individual lives, knowing that any good gift comes from Him (Jas. 1:17).

Fourth, God perfectly integrates our personal interactions with Him and our corporate interactions as a body to grow us in love. There seems to be a spiritual "springboard" effect that happens as we participate in both of these relational activities. Sometimes God gives us a personal experience of His love that helps us to receive or give love to others. At other times someone in the body may love us or give us grace that allows us to more deeply understand and receive the same from God Himself. For instance, we might come out of hiding with someone in the church by telling them a secret about our thoughts, feelings, or actions, and they listen to our story in grace and without condemnation. That experience can then encourage us to talk more freely with God about the needs of our hearts. Conversely, while pouring out our hearts to God in personal prayer, the Spirit might encourage us to share our story with someone with skin on, to grow in our transparency and trust of others in God's family.

God uses both our individual relationship and our body relationships as He sees fit, for our good. He knows that often we need the physical reality of His presence represented in another person who can weep with us, rejoice with us, hear our confession, pray for our healing, bear with us, forgive, love, instruct, encourage, and even reprove us in love. We need to know that others who love Jesus are for us, are committed to seek our good in Christ (Rom. 12: 9-21, Col. 3:12-17, Gal. 6:1). As we engage with one another, our spiritual responsibility is to point each other back to Jesus—to look to Him for healing, forgiveness, wisdom, and the saving grace and mercy that only He can provide for us individually and as a community.

When the Body of Christ functions together in the power and grace of Jesus and His Spirit, it is a glorious, beautiful, and astoundingly transformative community in which to abide. It affords us a glimpse of living together in eternity when all things will be in harmony with the love of Christ. I have been privileged to have some experiences with the body that felt a little like that. For a few years, I was blessed to abide in such a community. It wasn't made up of perfect people but rather of people committed to look together to and for Christ.

While journeying with those believers, I was able to be honest about my struggles, doubts, insecurities, and past hurts. I learned to listen to and give grace to others as they shared their stories and lives. We affirmed our mutual desire to find and follow God's will for us. We stood by each other through that process, knowing that it might extend longer than we wanted, traverse places in our hearts that we weren't expecting, and generally not be in our control. We were all committed to look to the Holy Spirit for direction and discernment as we traveled together.

That was a wonderful and transformative time for me. It changed me personally and also changed my vision for how the body can function. I long for more people in the church to experience the body in this way. Often, though, we come together as a body at various levels of understanding and engagement in our relationship with God. Although we might long to participate in a community that always acts like the ideals expressed in Scripture, our relational encounters can feel less than perfect.

Apprehension can rob us of the ability to entrust our hearts to God or to other Christians, or we might lack understanding about how we are supposed to get along. We may be looking to other people to fix our problems (or they might feel it is their mission to fix us) rather than going together to Christ to seek the solutions we need. We could be bringing hurts with us from other encounters with believers that have taught us to be wary. Many of us are hiding our real problems from each other, choosing to engage on superficial levels of sharing and caring, rarely speaking the truth to each other in love. Perhaps we feel lonely, even in the middle of a crowd of Christians.

How might God be inviting us to relationship even in the midst of that kind of body reality? Can He still use such an imperfect community for our good? I believe He can and He does.[2] God always meets us exactly where we are and invites us into relationship in our current circumstances. If we are willing to open our hearts to Him, to seek His wisdom and help, He can guide us through any encounter with other believers for His glory and the ultimate good of the body. For example,

» He uses other Christians, even those we find hardest to get along with, to invite us to love—to patiently engage with them, pray for them, and to look for how God is working in them. We have the opportunity to talk with God about these relationships, opening our hearts to the Spirit and what He is doing to help us grow.

» It is an ironic reality that those who we don't like very well are often capable of telling us truth about our hearts. Sometimes they see us more clearly than others whom we enjoy being with. If we listen to and then reflect on their observations about us with God, He may teach us something about ourselves, possibly some truth that we are avoiding.

» Our willingness to relate for the sake of Christ with those who rub us the wrong way might rub off some of our rough edges. Engaging with them can grow our capacity for patience and compassion.

---

2   If you are feeling alone or isolated in your spiritual journey right now, I want to take a minute and encourage you to pray and attentively look for a couple of believers at least who you can regularly share your life with, people you can risk trusting, people you suspect love Jesus and who desire for you to love Him as well. The group does not need to be big to give you an experience of community. You have a spiritual and relational need to connect with other believers, and it is good to ask God to supply that need. Ironically, you may be a leader in a church or in some other Christian organization. Your position may cause you to feel that there is no one with whom you can be honest and vulnerable. In your case it may be especially good for you to seek how God can provide a safe, loving, and supportive group of believers that can give the gift of community to you.

» Giving love to those who are difficult for us to love can invite them to a new experience of God's love for them. Through the process we might also need to receive God's love in deeper ways ourselves (1 John 4:19).

» In God's gracious mercy, He occasionally offers us the loveliest gift from unexpected places:

- a word of encouragement or prayer from the last person we would expect

- a gift of tangible support from a weaker brother

- help in time of need from someone who we thought was against us

The challenge for us in these situations is whether we can humble our hearts and receive these gifts. Are we able to encourage and contribute to the growth of our brother/sister by accepting their help? Are we willing to explore with God how we can give to them as well?

It is often the imperfect encounters in our relationships that offer perfect opportunities to grow in love. It is natural, even for the sinful, to only love those that are easy to love. However, Jesus asks us to learn to follow His example and also love those who act like our enemies (Luke 6:32-36). We can start this process by opening our hearts to how the Spirit is growing us in love for those in our spiritual family whom we find difficult to love. Also through Christ we can offer ourselves in relationship to those in the body who might find it difficult to love us as well!

Whatever our experience may currently be with the Body of Christ—whether we are deeply connected with other believers in community, living on the fringe of a church body, frustrated with other Christians in our lives, or going through the motions—apathetic to the whole idea of relating to other believers—Jesus is always calling us to deeper relationship and love within His family. If we are willing to embrace that call to love, He will always do more in us and through us than we could ask or think (Eph. 3:20).

PAUSE TO CONSIDER

» How has your experience with the Body of Christ affected your relationship with God? Has it helped you draw closer to God and grow in love? Or has it been more challenging?

» How did the descriptions above of the Body's role in our lives strike you? Did it make you excited about the possibilities; wistful for a past experience, skeptical as to whether this could be true, upset about a past hurt, grateful for your current experiences with God's people, or a mix of these? Talk with the LORD about whatever you discover.

» How might God be inviting you to engage with the Body of Christ right now? Are there specific actions He might be calling you to take? Take a moment to journal about it.

Chapter 10. Becoming a Follower of Jesus

But whatever gain I had, I counted as loss for the sake of Christ. Indeed, I count everything as loss because of the surpassing worth of knowing Christ Jesus my LORD. For his sake I have suffered the loss of all things and count them as rubbish, in order that I may gain Christ and be found in him, not having a righteousness of my own that comes from the law, but that which comes through faith in Christ, the righteousness from God that depends on faith— that I may know him and the power of his resurrection, and may share his sufferings, becoming like him in his death, that by any means possible I may attain the resurrection from the dead. Not that I have already obtained this or am already perfect, but I press on to make it my own, because Christ Jesus has made me his own. Philippians 3:7-12

As we conclude our reflection about our relationship with God and others in our lives, I want to end by exploring where this journey may lead. What is the end goal of intentionally deepening our relationships with God and others in the Body of Christ? Can love truly help us to become like Jesus, or might we only become more self-focused and absorbed?

This side of heaven, it is unlikely that our heart motivations will ever be completely pure. But if we seek to fall in love with God, our lives will be changed. Love will enliven our desire to find and follow the will of God. Isn't that what it means to live like Jesus (John 5:30, 8:28-29, 14:10)? Isn't that what we all want?

Isn't that what we all want? That is an important question to answer and the reason why learning to love Jesus is a journey of the heart. It requires that we explore with Jesus the attachments, fickleness, willfulness, independence, and other vestiges of sin that play unattended in our hearts. This journey happens through relationship as we allow the Spirit to teach us truth about the loveliness of Christ and about the neediness of our hearts, as we humbly learn to accept the enormity of Christ's love for us until we are filled with the fullness of God (Eph. 3:14-19).

The Apostle Peter's life is a pointed example of this process. For three years, Jesus developed a relationship with Peter as one of His disciples. Peter never seemed to lack passion in his responses to Jesus. The first time they met, the text says that Jesus looked at Peter and then changed his name from Simon to Cephas (Peter). Peter at once left his fishing business behind and went on the road with Christ. I wonder if part of his initial decision to follow Jesus was based on that name change—if Peter sensed right from the beginning that Jesus knew him better than he knew himself (John 1:41-42).

Through the course of their relationship, Christ's complete understanding of Peter would prove to be true. By the grace of God, Peter hung in there through the confusing times when other disciples turned away because they failed to understand Jesus's teaching; Peter, on the other hand, declared that he had nowhere else to go. He trusted that Jesus was the Christ even though he, too, likely didn't fully understand Christ's words (John 6:66-69).

Peter also stayed through the times when Jesus pointedly showed him the motivations of his heart. In one instance, Peter tried to quietly pull Jesus aside to rebuke Him for talking about His eventual death. He refused to accept these words from Christ. He didn't want Jesus to die. Jesus turned the tables on Peter and rebuked him in return. He confronted Peter with the truth that his heart was not focused on the things of God but rather was fettered by man's concerns. Peter's motivations were not only hindering their relationship but making it harder for Jesus to fulfill His mission. Peter needed to recognize that his heart had its own plans, and then decide if he was willing to surrender instead to the Father's plan, to be the follower that Jesus was calling him to be (Matt. 16:21-23).

When the time came for Jesus to die, Peter faced another truth about his heart. In his pride, he had overestimated his love for Jesus. He believed that he was prepared to follow Jesus all the way to death, to lay down his life for Christ. During Christ's trial for His life, Peter faced the shame of repeatedly denying his relationship with Jesus when people questioned him. But Jesus also knew this prideful part of Peter's heart. Christ encouraged him with the assurance that He had prayed for Peter's faith to survive his failure, and that Peter would eventually use his experience to strengthen others (Luke 22:31-34). Essentially, Jesus held onto Peter while Peter discovered his own inability to cling to Christ. Jesus interceded for their relationship; He stood by Peter while Peter's heart was struggling to accept the truth of his need.

Peter's life beautifully illustrates the gloriously messy, revealing, raw, and transformative relationship that Jesus offers each of us. This kind of relationship is the way of grace; this is the way to grow in love.

In the last chapter of John, we read of another conversation between Jesus and Peter after the resurrection. The topic is love, specifically the nature of Peter's love for Jesus. Because Peter had overestimated his love for Jesus in the past, it was important that he understood his relationship with Christ correctly. Through His questioning and in light of Peter's recent failure, Jesus invited Peter to explore the true quality of his love for Him, to admit that he needed to rely on what Jesus knew was true about his heart. He needed Jesus to help him figure out his heart issues and continue to grow in love.

The scene is an honest and intimate one between a man and his God. As Peter's love for Jesus is revealed through their encounter, it becomes apparent why Jesus initiated the conversation. Peter needed to know the level of his love for Jesus to go where Jesus was planning to lead him. Peter would have to rely on his relationship with Christ as he journeyed forward. In the end, Jesus made it simple for Peter to remember. He summed up their encounter with two words: follow me.

I think that is where a relationship with God leads us all. We grow to love and trust Him in deeper ways as we engage in conversation with Him about the needs in our lives, as we participate in relationship with others in the Body of Christ, as we read the Bible with our hearts attuned to the Spirit's work, as we grow in our capacity to discern God's loving movements on our hearts.

That love and trust allows us to follow Him authentically from our hearts. Where God chooses to lead us is completely up to Him. Our lives will likely become consumed with sharing His love with others who are lonely, hurting, and in need of the kind of love that only Jesus offers. We will engage in the work of inviting others to be reconciled with God—a relationship that has transformed our lives. Where that commission specifically takes each of us, only Jesus knows. When Peter asked Jesus if another disciple was being led to the same end as he, Jesus essentially told Peter that it was none of his business. He reiterated His command for Peter to be concerned only with whether he was following Jesus (John 21:20-23).

For now, we are left with a question. Do we love Him? In order to find out, like Peter, we need to actively engage in a relationship with Jesus. He is the only One who knows the true nature of our love. He is the only One who can help us grow to love Him more until we joyfully follow Him from the heart, wherever that may lead.

May "the grace of the LORD Jesus Christ and the love of God and the fellowship of the Holy Spirit be with you all" (2 Cor. 13:14).

PAUSE TO CONSIDER

» As you consider Peter's spiritual journey to grow in love, what aspects of his experience do you relate to? What aspects are hard for you to understand or identify with?

» Think about the question Jesus repeatedly asked Peter in John 21: "Do you love Me?" If Jesus were to ask you the same question, what would be your honest answer to Him?

» In light of what you've read in this book, consider your relationship with God. What might you want to express to the LORD? How might He be inviting you to respond?

LIVE INTO IT

Practice Opening Up to God

Spend 20 minutes talking with God about something that you've been hiding, either from Him, someone else or yourself. It could be a feeling, an action you took, a struggle you're facing or an opinion you hold. Notice how you feel before, during and after this open and honest conversation with God.

Practice Accepting God's Love Through Others

Spend 20 minutes accepting help from a fellow Christian. Ask a Christian you know to help you out in some way. Notice what it is like to receive God's love through the Body of Christ. Note whether this is easy or difficult for you.

Practice Loving Jesus

Spend 20 minutes focusing on Jesus. Express to Him the ways and degree to which you love Him, and the ways and degrees to which you love other things more than Him. Try to be as honest and open as you can in His presence. Give space for Jesus to respond to you. Note if He communicates to you through Scripture, the physical world, your circumstances or just a sense of His presence. Notice how you react to this encounter with Jesus.

NOTES

DISCUSS TOGETHER

What do you think?

Has your understanding of how we can actively participate in an ongoing and open relationship with God and the Body of Christ changed or expanded through this study?

How do you feel?

How do you feel about engaging in this kind of relationship with God and His people? What excites you? What makes you feel nervous or afraid?

What about God?

Has there been a recurring theme or particular idea that has caught your attention through this study? Take a few minutes to allow everyone to silently speak with God about this question, then let anyone share who wants to.

Where to go from here?

What would you like to remember and practice from this material? How would you like your relationships—with God and/or with others—to change?

NOTES

ACKNOWLEDGMENTS

In the last several years I have grown to appreciate and value God's gift of community in my life. In writing this book, I am grateful for how others came along side me and offered their support, wisdom, prayers and knowledge to contribute to its completion.

In particular, I would like to thank my editors: Ben Burkholder, Matthew Green, and Genalin Niere who took time to reflect on the writing and evaluate the theological and psychological implications, and Becky Miller and Autumn Swindoll for their copy edits.

To my staff, especially Monica Romig Green, who engaged with me in an ongoing conversation about the content, I am grateful for your insights and patience when the writing distracted me from other tasks.

Additionally, there were many who faithfully prayed through the process, notably my mother and my dear friend Dolores Elkins.

There is however only one person who lived with me during the journey, not just of writing this book but through the life-changing experiences that it chronicles—my husband Curt. There are no words to adequately convey the gratitude I feel for the gift of such a life partner. Thank you, honey, for being a demonstration of Christ's love for me. You have achieved the balance of holding me together while simultaneously releasing me to God and my journey with Him. I love you very much.

ABOUT GRAFTED LIFE

Grafted Life partners with church ministries to build relational cultures of love for God and one another.

We believe that, at its core, the Gospel of Jesus Christ is an invitation to radical relational transformation—the kind that exposes our habits of independence in order to embrace reliance on Christ and connection with His Body. God wants to do so much more than many Christians are experiencing, in our hearts, in our families, in our churches, and in our world—simply by making us whole relational beings who know how to give the kind of love that transforms others because we have learned to abide in His incredible love for us.

Grafted Life invites believers into deeper Christian life through intentional engagement with God and the Body of Christ. Whether participating in the *Life with God* journey or connecting one-on-one with a spiritual director, our resources encourage intimate, heart-probing, and transforming relationships with God and others.

We began in 2010 under the name Evangelical Center for Spiritual Wisdom (ECSW). Since then we have developed, tested, and distributed three kinds of resources for relational/spiritual development:

Free Online Resources

Through our website, individuals and churches can access:

- weekly reflections about connecting with God in real life
- articles on topics pertinent to relational/spiritual growth
- prayer exercises that practice Christian living
- book reviews and recommendations

In addition we produce *Witness*, a free monthly resource email written by Debbie Swindoll, executive director of Grafted Life. *Witness* serves Christian leaders and lay persons for their continued spiritual and relational growth.

Small Group Resources

The Art of Spiritual Leadership. This six week peer training is designed for any Christian leader, regardless of their ministry context or experience, and prepares them to cultivate small group communities that are spiritually focused and skillfully loving.

Life with God: A Journey of Relationship. *Life with God* is a 1-3 year discipleship curriculum that creates relationally capable people. Over six 12-week semesters, Christians break down barriers that exist across all of their relationships, including with God, within themselves, with other Christians, with friends and family members, and with their neighbors. Participants are guided by biblical teaching, the Holy Spirit, and a small group leader trained from within their community.

Do You Love Me? Group Study. This four week group experience explores the biblical foundation for relationship with God and one another. It is rich in personal illustration and invites individual reflection, practical application, and honest group discussion.

SPIRITUAL DIRECTION RESOURCES

Evangelical Spiritual Directors Association (ESDA) is an international association and the largest online directory of evangelical Christian spiritual directors.

Spiritual direction is a confidential one-on-one session with a trained spiritual director that explores how God is working in and through your life. Sessions may be arranged in-person, over the phone, or online. Hospitable and grounded in biblical truth, spiritual direction can help you grow in prayer and live into your calling as a follower of Christ.

ESDA member spiritual directors are a trustworthy resource to pastors and lay persons: formally trained listeners who ascribe to an ethical code and an evangelical creed. ESDA provides professional support to member spiritual directors as well as a platform for promotion and access to the ministry of spiritual direction in evangelical environments.

Contact Us

We would love to hear about your experience with *Do You Love Me?* Contact us with your questions or comments.

Website: www.graftedlife.org
Email: info@graftedlife.org

CPSIA information can be obtained
at www.ICGtesting.com
Printed in the USA
BVHW080952030820
585324BV00001B/182

9 781732 874701